Increase Profit From your Florist Shop

THE SMALL BUSINESS SUCCESS GUIDE

Copyright © 2015 Brendan Power

All rights reserved.

ISBN: 1508518742
ISBN-13: 978-1508518747

DEDICATION

To small business owners everywhere.

CONTENTS

	Why do you need this book?	1
1	The profit in sales techniques	4
2	Look like a million dollars	8
3	Chewing up the profits	17
4	Paper money	21
5	More sales, less budget	34
6	Small cost, big impact	54
7	Make money answering the telephone	67
8	Time is money	70
9	Social money	72
10	Right on the money	76
	The buck stops here	80
	References	81

WHY DO YOU NEED THIS BOOK?

Do you want to increase the profit you make from your florist business?

Do you want some easy to follow tips for business success? Yes? Well you have come to the right place.

In this book you will find easy tips and tricks to improve your sales and profitability. And it all starts with your marketing.

Marketing covers everything aspect of your business, not just your advertising. It covers the quality of your product and the way you answer the phone. Your marketing will make you stand out from your competition. It will produce customer loyalty by providing a great experience as well as delivering a great product.

With just a few small and easy changes, a few minutes of a day you can turn your florist into a small business success story.

The three principles of a successful florist business are.

- Cultivate
- Grow
- Thrive

CULTIVATE

The first three chapters of this book will help you cultivate your existing business. You will find tips and tricks to increase your sales (and your profit) from your existing customers. There is no point adding new customers if you cannot look after the ones you already have.

GROW

Chapter's four to nine discuss advertising and promotion methods to grow your customer base and improve customer loyalty. You will learn about guerrilla marketing techniques and how to apply them to your florist. Social media, television, radio and the more traditional flyers and newsletters are all covered in detail. There are ideas for all budgets, but mostly for small budgets.

THRIVE

The last chapter deals with managing your business for long term success.

What are you waiting for? Start growing your business now!

CULTIVATE
Create an environment to sell as much as possible to customers already coming to your store.

1 THE PROFIT IN SALES TECHNIQUES
Sell more to your existing customers

Did you know it costs less to sell to your existing customers then it does to gain new customers? In fact it costs five to seven times more to gain new customers than it does to retain them.

How do you sell more to your existing customers? Improve your sales techniques. Without gaining any new customers or incurring any marketing expenses, you can sell more.

You can follow all the strategies outlined later in this book and increase the amount of people coming to your store. But if you cannot sell them anything, all your time, effort and money has been wasted.

Sales techniques are a combination of different processes and skills that successful sales people use.

In this chapter you will find the following sales techniques:
- Understand how a buyer makes the decision to buy
- Catch the sales that slip through
- How to help the customer, rather than sell to the customer.
- Start improving your selling techniques now!

1. GREET YOUR CUSTOMER
Greet your customer warmly on entering your store. Many shoppers complain they are never greeted on entering a store.

2. EYE CONTACT
Display a sincere interest in helping the customer. A significant 72% of shoppers complain that sales assistants do not make eye contact when speaking to a customer, and appear to be bothered when the customer asks a question.

3. HELP PEOPLE BUY
Salesmen: love them or loathe them, they are a necessity. Without

salespeople, businesses do not exist and established businesses can fail.

But not everyone is a natural at sales, some need extra help. Take a look at the following example.

Have you ever walked into a store to browse, only to have the assistant comment on every single garment that you pull off the rack? Sure, the assistant is doing their job. But is it effective? What do you, as buyer, feel towards this person who watches your every move and tries to sell you everything you look at: warmth or irritation? Does this happen in your store?

Sales are not a matter of the seller telling the person to buy. There is information that must be exchanged. The exchange of information is called communication. And, as every successful salesperson will tell you, communication is what sales is all about.

Patrick Forsyth, of Marketing on a Tight Budget,[1] has identified seven stages that the buyer's mind goes through on the way to making a purchase:

- I am important and I want to be respected.
- Consider my needs.
- How will your ideas help me?
- What are the facts?
- What are the snags?
- What shall I do about them?
- I approve.

For the sale to be effective, salesperson needs to be familiar with each of these stages in decision making, and be able to respond to each stage satisfactorily. If there is a breakdown somewhere along this path, chances are the buyer will not feel confident, will hesitate, and will walk away, without the purchase.

Note that these steps and their responses involve a two way flow of communication between the buyer and the seller. It is NOT one sided.

4. ARE YOU LISTENING?

Telling is not selling. Selling is listening.

Actively listen your way to success by asking good question. Listen and attempt to understand the answers and the questions you get from your customers.

5. APPROACH ME

Be approachable and quietly chatty, without overpowering your customers. Remember the above stages, use them in sequence and in step with the buyer, and sell the benefits.

Using this technique should see more sales being made, more repeat business, and more profit.

6. IT IS NOT WHAT YOU SAY BUT HOW YOU SAY IT

Research has shown that clients are more likely to be positively influenced by the salesperson whose speech patterns are similar to their own.[2]

When speaking with your next client, modify your own speech patterns to fit with theirs. For example, you are talking with your client and you notice that their natural speech pattern is slower and the volume is softer than yours. You should respond by slowing down your speech and softening your volume to match. By doing so you will find that your words are more thoroughly understood and your message or advice is clearer, resulting in a greater likelihood that you will get the initial sale and retain this client's repeat business.

When you first greet your client, remember to listen out for their speech patterns and try to fit in with them.

7. CATCHING THE SALES THAT SLIP THROUGH

Do you find sales seem to slip through your fingers? Let us have a look at what could be going wrong.

The optimum way of selling is to adhere to the following sequence.

- The retailer needs to recognize and cater to the customer's need to feel important and respected.
- Next, the retailer should cater to the customer's specific need and provide ideas that will help them.
- Give them the facts, the snags, advice and your approval of the purchase.

Missing out one of those stages will affect whether or not a sale goes through. Sometimes the seller progresses through the stages out of step with the buyer. The seller must not work through the sequence too quickly or too slowly for the buyer.

8. SELL BENFITS NOT PRODUCT

Perhaps you sold the product, the flowers, rather than the benefits to the buyer.

When selling any product, it is essential to remember that customers' buying decisions are based primarily on what benefits the product derives. Always emphasize the benefits your flowers will provide, rather than the price or the flowers themselves.

Flowers are not a staple item. They are a pleasure, a joy, and a luxury. On some occasions the buyer has no real need to buy flowers, but the benefits of the flowers, spelt out to the customer, are what will actually the sale.

9. HELP NOT SELL

Most people can spot a salesperson a mile away. And once they have spotted one, what do they do? Walk the other way, look down, and put up the old "Do not try to sell me anything" wall. So how do you sell your stock to these people? Shift the focus. Do not sell, help.

Most customers want to enjoy a friendly relationship with store owners.

In an era of automated, online everything, customers need to feel that they count. They will be attracted to the human element. After product, customers want service.

What customer service means to the customer (not the salesperson) is someone who is interested in them as an individual. So chat to the customer without being nosey.

A way of doing this is to move the focus away from selling and on to your own experiences. Talk about what has been happening in your own life first, then gradually move to the customer's life. Once a rapport has been established, they will open up. When the lines of communication are open, you will be able to change the focus back to the flowers, with a much greater chance of making a sale.

Once a customer has decided to buy some flowers you will be able to value-add the service. This is when you can suggest accessories such as cards or vases. Not only will they help make the sale of the major item but they will add to the total dollar value of the sale. In addition, you will be seen as knowledgeable while giving a caring, intimate touch to the sale process.

10. EGO - IT IS NOT A DIRTY WORD

No-one's ego can be fed enough. Always compliment your customer's appearance. Act as though you are interested in what they tell you about their lives. Be tactful in the way you do this. Try not to come across as superficial.

11. AFTER SALES SERVICE

Help your customers take care of their cut flowers. Discourage less effectual do-it-yourself tricks for floral preservation. Instead offer them professional tips on how to preserve their flowers correctly.

12. THANK YOU

After making a sale, always follow up with a thank you note or e-mail, and include advertisements for future in store promotions. More about promotions later in this book.

13. POSITIVES ATTRACT

Personalities are contagious. If your attitude is positive, your customers' will be too. Positive attitudes make sales.

CHAPTER SUMMARY

This chapter covered of basic sales techniques including:
- Help people buy
- Catching the sales that slip through
- How to help the customer, rather than sell to the customer.

End of chapter one (1)

2 LOOK LIKE A MILLION BUCKS
Tips for a good looking store

You have improved your sales techniques and have seen an increase in sales from your existing customers. You know if you get the customers in the door, you stand a good chance of making a sale. So the next logical step would be to spend money on some advertising and promotions.

Not yet!

Before you spend any money on advertising or promotions, ask yourself: could the look and feel of your store be putting customers off?

If the customer does not walk through the front door, how can you use your selling techniques?

You can follow all the strategies outlined later in this book and increase the amount of people coming to your store. But if they get to the front door and do not like what they see, they will not come into your store. And if they do not come in, you have wasted your time, effort and money on advertising and promotions.

In this chapter you will find hints, tips and tricks on how to create a good looking store that will encourage your customer to buy! You will learn:

- How to look the part from the outside
- What makes a good looking sign
- Your window of opportunity
- How to look the part from the inside.

Time to get better looking!

14. BECOME A SUPER SLEUTH

A major part of being in business involves keeping an eye on your competitor. Become a detective and check out your competition on their home turf. Make your business image better than theirs.

Put on that spy hat and scope out the competition with the aid of the following checklist.

- Do a drive past and note:
- Are the premises easy to spot from the car as you pass?
- Are they clean and well maintained?
- Is the sign easy to read? Does it clearly state that the business is a florist?
- Are business hours posted?
- Is the door open? Or, with air-conditioned stores, does the store look open?
- Does the business look successful?
- Would you be inclined to go in?
- What is the neighbourhood like? Is it busy and prosperous, neat or run-down?
- Does the shop seem to suit the area?
- Is public transport available and convenient?
- What are the people on the street wearing?
- What types of cars are in the neighbourhood?
- Is parking available and are the parking lots full?
- What strikes you immediately? Write a few notes and describe your first impression of the business. What strikes you immediately (think visuals, smells and sounds)?

After you have driven past, go in and make note of the following:

- What is your immediate reaction on entering the store?
- Describe the atmosphere. Is there music playing, or is it clinically quiet?
- If there is music playing, is it appropriate?
- Is the room neat and clean or cluttered, spacious or cramped?
- Is the attendant occupied and busy? Is a professional and caring image presented to the waiting customers?
- Do the staff wear uniforms and/or present an appropriate impression of the store?
- Are they knowledgeable and helpful?

Apply what you have learnt about your competitors to your shop twice as well!

15. SUPER DUPER SLEUTHING

Attending trade shows can prove very beneficial to your business. In addition to viewing products, you can gather information, scope out your competitors, and establish and improve communication with manufacturing companies.

16. STAFF SLEUTHING

Provide your staff with opportunities to attend trade shows and seminars. It is a great way to stimulate employee productivity, increase the amount of expertise, and decrease voluntary turnover.

17. LOOK THE PART

Looking the part is all about the customer committing your shop to memory and then recalling it when necessary.

Take every opportunity you can to advertise your business. A uniform will advertise your outlet almost free of charge. The sight of your staff in their characteristic clothing as they walk to and from work or while delivering stunning floral arrangements will stamp your store in the minds of the buying public.

You can coordinate your uniform with any other form of advertising you use. This works particularly with color. A combination of colors is instantly recognizable and promotes good memory recall.

The use of a running theme as a constant reminder of your business is also beneficial. Select your uniform, the colors, the car decorations, the advertising in newspapers and magazines, the memento or business card, the tag on the bunch of flowers at the local dental surgery. And make them all the same. This becomes a cost-efficient way to spend your advertising dollar. In addition, the running theme will give your business a corporate look, making your enterprise look strong, stable and established.

18. LOOK, STICK WITH IT

Consider the style of your business

- Find a uniform that suits your personality, your target audience and your style of business.
- Try a gimmick. Be creative.
- Wear a hat decorated with flowers. Adorn your shoes with rosebuds.
- Don a corsage. Choose a floral fabric for a skirt/blouse/dress/shirt/scarf/tie.
- Or try a more executive look by sticking with particular blocks of color.

Two very powerful tools are the visual image and color. Both are easily retained in peoples' memories. Make good use of this and stick with your color choice or theme.

19. BE WHO YOU WANT TO BE

To function well in business, your establishment needs an identity. You will create your identity by choosing the decor and the staff who work for you.

Like attracts like, Birds of a feather flock together, there are many sayings that describe the fact that people like to be with others who are like themselves and who belong to the same socioeconomic class. Acknowledge this fact so you can define your market and give your establishment an identity.

How do your customers know whether they fit in? They stand out the front of your store and look inside. They check out the staff, what they look like, what they are wearing, their demeanor and their attitude. The warmth and friendliness of your staff will tip the hesitant customer over the line to commit to entering your store.

20. WELCOME

Ensure your staff members greet regular customers by name; ensure they welcome strangers; make sure customers are not left standing too long unattended; and make sure all your staff wear a smile and a stylish uniform.

Make it your mission to ensure all these things come together to provide a complete picture, where each facet supports the other to create the identity you want. This will project a solid image that leaves no doubt in the mind of the customer that yours is the florist they will feel comfortable in.

21. STAY TIDY

Aim to maintain a pleasant shopping atmosphere. Dirty, cluttered and untidy wrap desks, benches or displays are all things that can unfavorably influence a customer's decision to return.

22. WHAT WAS YOUR NAME AGAIN?

Is the name of your business letting you down?

- A catchy name is an important marketing tool.
- It needs to be easy to remember and easy to say.
- A double meaning often works well because the cleverness and wit stick in people's minds.
- Match the tone of the name with the image you would like to project.

23. GIVE ME A SIGN

Your sign is important. It is your hardest working employee. Your sign works 24 hours a day, seven days a week. It tells everybody who passes who you are and where you are. But is it letting your business down?

Is your sign in good condition?

- Is it faded, weathered, crackling or peeling? You are selling fresh flowers, so you need a fresh sign.
- Is it stable?
- Does it look professional?
- Is it easy to read? Is there enough contrast between the letters and the background?
- Are the color scheme and style current? While it is not generally considered good practice to change the style of your sign on a regular basis, do check that it is current. You want your

customers to know that you are up to date.
- How does you signage compare with other businesses around you?
- Do the colors catch your attention, or do they blend in with all the other signs in the vicinity?

24. BANNER

Your sign also includes the banner that you can periodically hang out the front of your shop.

Remind customers that Valentine's Day is 14 February. Name the actual day of the week, to stop any further confusion.

The concept applies, of course, to Mothers' Day, as well as any individual promotions that you might run.

25. SIGN LANGUAGE

The most effective signs are one to three words in length and usually no more than six words long. The message should be short, sharp and concise

Your sign should be in keeping with your advertising theme, to optimize customers' recall of the ads for your business that they have already seen.

The rules of signs:
- Limit the sign to a few words, usually no more than six.
- Keep a contrast in color between the background and the lettering.
- Stick to one print type.
- Keep the print type simple (not fancy), so it is easy to read.

How much information should you put on your sign? Customers spend, on average, less than two seconds looking at a sign. So they need to be able to get the message in an instant. Use only a few words.

Remember: Keep It Simple, Sweetheart.

26. PERSUASIVE

What are the most persuasive words?

Research has determined the most persuasive words in the English language are:
- you,
- money,
- easy,
- safety,
- save,
- new,
- love,
- discovery,
- proven,
- guarantee,

- health,
- results.

Others to add to the list are free, sale, now, yes, benefits, announcing.
Use these words, where you can, in your signs.

27. A GOOD LOOKING SIGN

What makes a sign look good?

Pictures. As the saying goes, "a picture is worth a thousand words". Pictures are fast communicators and attention grabbers. If your sign is small, concentrate on the words and drop the picture.

Lettering style. Light lettering against a dark background or vice versa will give you a sign that is easy to read. The words need to be large and should be printed in a single font. Keep the actual lettering style clear. Avoid fancy, difficult-to-read fonts.

Colors. While color coordination is good for floral arrangements, it is not good for signs. Maintain contrast in colors on the actual sign itself, and make sure that the signs do not blend into your existing decor or get lost among the myriad colors presented by the flowers themselves.

No other signs. If there are too many signs to look at, the potential buyer will switch off. A bombardment of signs all competing for the customers' attention is the visual equivalent of shouting at them.

Correct spelling. Incorrect spelling does not make you look good. The only exception is if it is a deliberate play on words.

Punctuation is not necessary. Often a sign will not use a full sentence anyway. And punctuation can clutter the picture. Commas and full stops are not essential. The exclamation mark is good to use because it lends an air of excitement and commands the attention of the reader.

28. POINT OF SALE SIGNS

If you need to place signs in your store, the best placement is that which interrupts the natural sightlines in a given area. Be the customer. Walk into your store and stand there. Take note of where you are looking. That is where you put your sign

Your point-of-sale signs are an inexpensive way to improve your profit. They:

- act as silent salespeople,
- direct the consumer to purchase.
- encourage impulse buying.
- plant the seeds for future buying.

Use them whenever you can!

29. NEWS BULLETIN

Bulletin boards are an inexpensive way to remind patrons where you are and what you can offer them. They can be a very effective way of attracting the eye of the person who is "Just looking, thanks".

30. WINDOW OF OPPORTUNITY

Does your front window do you justice?

- Is the glass clean?
- Is it bursting with color and life? Or are you going for a restrained, chic understatement?
- Do you have posters in your window advertising what you can offer?
- Are there too many posters in your window that detract from the beauty of the arrangements and create a cluttered effect?
- Is the approach to the shop clear and inviting?
- Is the door easily accessible and easily seen? Is it clean?
- Do you have too many A-frame signs near the doorway?

Could you try a few bouquets of flowers at the doorway to lure in the passer-by? Why not try a selection of cheap, cheerful bouquets to catch the eye of the impulse buyer?

Use your window. Look like a florist. Let people see the flowers. Advertise your promotion on a poster on the window in a spot that intercepts their sightline as they look at the flowers while standing waiting for the bus or as they walk past.

31. LET THERE BE LIGHT

Lighting must be bright enough to allow customers to see the actual colors of the flowers and their freshness and quality. It should not be too bright, though, so that the effect is clinical and unwelcoming.

32. MUSIC TO MY EARS

Music can be relaxing, inviting you to stay in the store longer. A sense of relaxation and the sheer fact that they have spent an extended amount of time in the shop can mean that the customer is more likely to buy.

Music appreciation is a matter of individual appeal, so go the middle ground. Happy music is what you need, nothing aggressive or too depressing. Relaxation/nature and classical music are safe options.

33. COMPLEMENT YOUR BUSINESS

Can you add retail products that complement the floral component of the business?

Choose gift lines, decor items and mementos that fit in with the flowers, as these are the mainstay of the business. Their sale will attract the impulse buyer or the person looking for something special and therefore boost your profit margins.

Conversely, are you stocking too many different types of items?

If you spread your retail base too thinly you will create a hotchpotch effect for the buyer. This will clutter the store and confuse the buyer. Find a focus and stay within its boundaries.

34. CROWDED HOUSE

If the customers can barely walk through the store without knocking things over, they will feel uncomfortable being there. Particularly if they have other parcels or children with them.

Alternatively, if there does not appear to be much to choose from, customers will not return.

35. ARE YOU UP TO DATE?

- Are your Christmas decorations still up in February? Take them down now!
- Do you have promotional advertisements in-store for upcoming occasions?
- Does your store look well maintained or does it have a tired, jaded, uncared-for feel? Ask a few friends for their honest opinion.
- Are your store decor items up to date? Wall hangings and pictures change styles fairly rapidly. There is nothing worse than being able to date a business by looking at the decor.
- Is your color scheme up to date?
- Does your logo look dated? Again, compare with other businesses to get a feel for what is current.

Check your business image once a year to stay current.

36. CONSISTENT DESIGN

The interior of your shop should be a theme that is going to complement what you sell and create a positive atmosphere. Make sure the theme runs through the entire shop, and aim to stick to one theme at a time.

37. WRAP TO IMPRESS

Packaging reinforces the quality of your products and, the idea of who you are. However, due to the usual tight budget of small business the quality of packaging is often overlooked.

In the floristry industry the quality of packaging also denotes whether the consumer keeps the flowers in the packaging or takes it off to put the bouquet in a vase. If the wrapping is attractive enough to make them keep it on, you have achieved further advertising in the customer's home. Your packaging will continue to advertise your services until the flowers are finally thrown away.

The quality of wrap and the way you package bouquets creates a certain look and image for your business. Obviously, different looks will appeal to different markets. Upmarket packaging, like the bouquets themselves, tends to be sleek and understated. Budget packaging is often more colorful and cheerful.

The packaging is going to help create different images for your business.

What is the competition doing? Are they more contemporary than you? The message is that everything communicates something about your product, including your packaging.

Packaging does not have to be expensive. It should be creative and emphasize quality. After buying a bouquet of flowers you want customers to feel good about their purchase. This will result in repeat purchases.

Try some of the following suggestions:
- Brown paper and raffia ties create a country and natural feel.
- Bold colored cellophane creates a suave and sophisticated image.
- Bright boxes and thick, colored ribbons create a contemporary feel.

If your packaging stands out when people are walking down the street with it, it can act as its own kind of advertising. McDonald's and Starbucks have focused on their packaging to successfully reinforce their brand over the years. Even their litter is advertising!

Potential customers will also perceive the quality of your business and products based on the quality of your packaging. Your package could be the first exposure of your product, so it needs to make a favorable impression.

CHAPTER SUMMARY

This chapter covered how to make your store look good and entice customers to visit and purchase. It covered:
- How to look the part from the inside
- What makes a good looking sign
- Your window of opportunity
- How to look the part from the inside

End of chapter two (2).

3 CHEWING UP THE PROFIT
Are your bad habits turning your customers off?

Your business is looking sharp from the outside and you have improved your sales techniques. You want to impress your clients. Have you considered that some of your mannerisms and your store behaviors might be doing your business more harm than good?

In this chapter you will find a list of habits that could be discouraging your customers from spending their money with you.

When you have finished reading this chapter, you should have an understanding of the following:

- Bad habits that could turn your customer off
- Staff enthusiasm and how it affects your customers

Time to change your habits!

38. CLEAN AND ORDERED

Is your studio clean and ordered at all times throughout the business day? It is not good enough to leave the cleaning and putting away until the end of the day. You never know when a customer will just walk in off the street. You must be prepared. Your store must be clean. Establish a routine where everybody is responsible for cleaning up after themselves and putting equipment and products away where they belong.

39. WHAT IS THAT SMELL

Do you or your staff smell like a cigarette? This is a big turn off for most customers. Ensure staff do not stand around the front of your store smoking. If you or your staff must smoke, make sure this is done away from customers' view. Ensure hands are washed and breath is fresh before returning to work.

40. DO NOT TURN YOUR CLIENT OFF

Are you turning your clients off? Here are some other things to avoid

doing in front of customers:
- chewing gum,
- eating and drinking,
- using sloppy speech and grammar,
- telling dirty jokes; foul language,
- holding religious discussions and debates; and
- gossiping about customers and staff.

Ensure:
- your staff members are aware of these standards.
- you model them.
- you enforce them.

41. DOUBLE NEGATIVE

Get rid of negative thinkers and negative philosophies. They have no place in your business and should never be allowed to come into contact with your customers.

42. AN EXTRA PAIR OF HANDS

Are you understaffed? Are customers waiting too long to be served or even acknowledged when they enter your store?

Would an extra pair of hands help? What about a free pair of extra hands?

By coordinating with schools and government employment training programs, you can use your store as a venue for the unskilled or for high school students to learn retail and people skills. There are advantages for both parties. The school or work skill organization gains a venue through which they can train people, and your business has extra staffing, for no monetary outlay.

Giving people the chance to work in your florist business gives them the opportunity to learn valuable skills. You can train people in many areas of your business, such as:
- flower design and arranging,
- customer service,
- marketing developing newsletters, designing ads etc.,
- cash budgeting and management.

Such a scheme not only generates extra staffing but can also result in publicity and positive word-of-mouth for your business. If it is a school program (i.e. work experience or placement during school hours) you could even receive exposure in the school newsletter. Free advertising for you! If you do run such a program, be sure to let your local community newspaper know. They may want to profile your store, meaning more exposure for your business!

To run this program takes only a little of your time and some initial organization. You are also giving your time back to the community, which is a highly commendable thing to do. Your community backing is a sure way to bring the community's support back to your business.

43. STAFF ENTHUSIASM

The attitude in your workplace greatly affects how the customers interact and whether they keep walking through the door. As Emerson said, "Nothing great was ever achieved without enthusiasm". The key is staff enthusiasm. Do they have it? Are they enjoying their job? Or is it merely something to pay the rent each week? What is their motivation? Are you encouraging them?

Staff need a reason to want to come to work. The solution is to make them feel important and valued, creating a sense of ownership of your business's outcomes. Praise and reward them when all goes well, and offer constructive feedback when problems arise.

Set goals. Give staff something to strive for. Sales goals and targets that have rewards attached will create motivation.

Offer training and skills development. Your staff should feel as if they are the best equipped in their industry. Ongoing training also lets your staff see that they are important to the business and that their contribution is valued; it gives them a sense of pride and credibility in the job that they are doing.

Equipping staff and stimulating enthusiasm is something that will flow through to customers. Genuine enthusiasm is contagious.

44. SHOW YOUR APPRECIATION

When your employees feel appreciated, they perform better at work. Providing meals for employees, especially when they work late, is always appreciated.

45. FEEDBACK

Your employees need constant feedback and encouragement on how they are doing in their jobs. They need to be aware of their good and bad points and feel comfortable discussing work performance issues with you.

46. LUXURY

Flowers are essentially a luxury item. Your attitude towards the customer needs to reflect the pampering and respect they are treating themselves to by deciding to purchase such gorgeous flowers.

CHAPTER SUMMARY

This chapter covered the mannerisms and behaviors that might be doing your business more harm than good. It covered:

- Bad habits that could turn your customer off
- Staff enthusiasm and how it affects how the customers in your store.

End of chapter three (3).

GROW
Increase the number of customers visiting your store

4 PAPER MONEY
Make money with direct mail, flyers, newsletters and business cards

Your business is looking sharp from the outside; you have improved you sales techniques and eliminated bad behaviors. Now it is time to get your name out there!

In this chapter you will find hints, tips and tricks on the following topics:

- Who to market to?
- How to market using flyers, newsletters and business cards.
- How to market using your invoice.
- How to personalise your marketing.
- How to stand out from your competitors.

Time to start getting your name out there!

47. IN THE BEGINNING

Advertising, promotions and publicity is a waste of time unless you target it at a specific group (called a target market). Take time to select your correct target market. A clear vision of your target market will allow you to target your marketing and promotions to reach your most promising prospects.

Defining a target market will not limit your business. New business owners sometimes resist defining a target market, thinking it will reduce the number of potential customers. Not so.

Identifying target customers does not prevent your business from accepting customers that do not fit the target profile. If such a customer seeks your product or service, you will still be available. But you have not spent any time, effort or money in the hope that customer walks through your door.

How to Define Your Target Market

When you identify your target market you are simply identifying the specific characteristics of the people (or businesses) you believe are most likely to buy your flowers.

Common characteristics used to classify customers include:

- age
- gender
- income level
- buying habits
- occupation or industry
- marital status
- family status (children or no children)
- geographic location
- ethnic group
- political affiliations or leanings, and
- hobbies and interests.

Use these criteria to draw a profile of your target market.

As a florist you may target women aged 25 to 55years old who live, within a ten mile radius of the store.

You can also target businesses within 10 miles of the store.

There is nothing wrong with targeting two different types of customers. When you plan to target two different types of customers you can plan promotions relevant to each customer.

48. WHY DO YOU PROMOTE?

The reason you promote your florist and its services is to gain more customers and retain them. So aim your promotions at customers you think you will be able to keep. Aim at the customers who will return, who will revisit on a regular basis, who will refer your services to others, and who will market your business for you because they, the customers, look good and hold reputable and prominent positions in the community.

Many customers will simply take the benefit of the promotion (i.e. the discount) and never come back. Some people skip from one store to another just to take advantage of a sale. This is a fact of life; it will always happen to some extent, no matter what you do. The trick is to minimize this occurrence. How?

Get the names and contact details of those who responded to the promotion and add them to your database. When you have done this, your promotion will achieve what it is designed to do:

- Not only will customers become aware of your store through your marketing, they will be given a reason to attend.

- Once they are in the door you have the opportunity to sell your service and your flowers.
- Having met the new customer and having already provided them a service, you now have reason to contact them.
- Contact them just before Mother's Day to check whether they were pleased with their arrangement.
- Contact them say, just before Valentine's Day to thank them for their custom.

49. RELEASE ME

A press release is one of the first publicity tools you should use. It is inexpensive, and when written correctly can be very effective. It announces the opening of your business, giving valuable coverage, and conveys your professionalism and enthusiasm.

Send a press release to every magazine or newsletter that is connected or relevant to your business in some way.

When planning a press release about your business, keep it simple, to the point, relevant and professional.

How do you write a press release? There are many free resources available on the internet to help you write your first press release.

50. ADVERTISING KEEPSAKES

Do you cut out and keep the ads you have placed in the newspaper and save them in a scrapbook? Great! But you should keep your own ads, and everyone else's, including your competitors'. Actually, you should keep the whole newspaper or magazine for future reference.

Quite often the proprietor and the advertising placer get into a routine because it is easy, safe and familiar. But is the ad actually working? Is it in the best position in the newspaper?

Look back and analyze your competitors' advertisements. How they advertised, what they advertised, and in what part of the newspaper they advertised. Now use the same criteria on your own advertisement.

Does the newspaper have an editorial section that could complement your business? The segment on weddings would be an obvious choice for a florist. Are there any others?

Do your competitors advertise in these sections? Are their businesses successful? Is it worth following their lead?

If you advertise only spasmodically or for special occasions, buy the newspaper or magazine many times before placing the ad. Decide on the best placement for your ad. Note how other companies are advertising.

51. BE DIFFERENT FROM THE OTHERS

Using the advertising keepsakes gathered above; note how your competitors are advertising. Then be different!

Use:

- a different font
- a different layout,
- a different orientation.

Your target market may not notice you simply because your ad looks like everyone else's or, worst of all, is being confused with your competitors' ads.

52. ADVERTISING CHECKLIST

- Does your advertisement stand out, or do you have to search the newspaper to find it? For an independent opinion, try giving the paper to an unsuspecting friend who was not a participant in the design or placement of the ad.
- Does your ad have a similar look to other ads in the newspaper? Could your business be confused with someone else's?
- How does your ad look in comparison with your competitors'? Does it look like a poor cousin?
- Is it placed in a section that will draw your target audience? (E.g. near related editorial, such as wedding, restaurant, or hospital promotions)?
- Does the look of your ad reflect the style of your store and therefore target and attract the market you are catering for?

53. COMPARISON ADS

A comparison ad can work very effectively for your business comparing the before and after of what buying flowers can do for the customer's relationship. But what is it?

A comparison ad will visually show potential customers what flowers from your business can do for them. Using a before and after approach can clearly indicate how flowers from your business will change the current state of a relationship. In two distinctive pictures placed side by side, create a before situation to the left and an after situation to the right. Above the pictures use a humorous headline.

For example, you could use The Mother in Law from Hell for a headline. In the before picture have an older woman with an evil look in her eye. The after picture could have the son in law handing her a bouquet of flowers and a very pleased looking mother in law.

Or you might headline the before and after pictures The Late Husband. Before, shows a woman sitting alone looking at the clock which says 9 pm, with a plate of cold food in front of her. She is waiting for her husband to come home. After, shows the husband walking through the door with a bunch of flowers; the wife smiles from ear to ear with arms outstretched.

You could tagline the whole campaign with the one slogan, something along the lines of "Jenny's Flowers, changing and enhancing relationships since 2008".

The benefits of this type of ad include:
- The pictures reinforce mentally what the purchase of the service will actually achieve.
- It alerts your customer to the necessity to do something (e.g. the mother-in-law).
- This type of advertising is very effective in flyers or newspaper ads.
- You may include a price reduction to further cinch the deal.

Remember, a picture communicates 1000 words. You can experiment with as many different situations as you like. Try grandparents, brothers and sisters, the boss; the list is endless. This type of ad can literally put you right into the consumers' relationship situations, highlighting the necessity and convenience of buying flowers from you.

54. BACK TO SCHOOL

Every parent who has a child at school knows they have to search their son's or daughter's school bag once a week to fish out the school newsletter. How many students are there at the local schools in your area? How many parents? How many homes and workplaces? How many relatives and friends do these people have, and how many potential settings for your gorgeous flowers does that make? What a wonderful source of potential clients right under your nose!

Some schools provide a page where business owners may buy space by the semester to advertise on the back page or pages of their newsletter. If the schools in your area have already done this, jump onto the bandwagon. Once parents have used your flower shop and been pleased with your work, you can be certain the word will spread. And it will be reinforced the next time their friend picks up the newsletter, only to see your ad.

If your neighborhood schools do not have this system in place, approach them and suggest they try it. Provide them with your business card to reprint, or design your own ad. Talk money, and they will probably acquiesce.

55. STAND OUT FROM THE CROWD

Flyers are an effective marketing tool. They can be dropped in mailboxes, handed out in the street, inserted in newspapers. Many businesses use flyers. But have you wondered whether your flyer gets lost in a sea of other people's flyers and mail outs? Well, of course it does!

However, if only 2% of the 1000 flyers you hand out results in a purchase, you have secured 20 purchases. And if your average price per bunch of flowers is $25, then you have made $500. If you distribute 5000 flyers, you might make $2500!

But remember to make your flyer stand out from the crowd. Study the examples you find in your own mailbox. Analyze the ones you get handed in the street. Avoid looking like all the other flyers. Especially avoid looking like your competitor.

Here are some tips to help your flyer stand out from the crowd.

- What color paper do the other businesses use? Try an alternative
- What print color? Use another.
- Do they have a picture? If they do, try going without- and vice versa.
- Is there an attention grabbing headline? This is a necessity for everyone.
- Is there too much information? Another important point for all flyers: do not crowd the space.
- Is there too little information?
- Have you provided a reason for people to patronise your store? Make sure you do!
- What size are the other flyers? Try a different size of paper.
- Does your paper have a fold? If so, make creative use of the fold try placing your attention grabber on the outside to entice the reader to open it and to read on. The word "FREE" printed on the outside fold will certainly create interest.

Good design in your flyer will ensure that these aims are achieved, and you will be on your way to making more profit.

56. WAITING FOR THE FLOWERS TO GROW

Handing out flyers on a street corner means you have to approach people and offer them your advertisement. What if you could entice people to ask you for your flyer?

The solution: offer them something for free, attached to your flyer. Staple a packet of seeds to your standard flyer. Then arouse their curiosity with the headlines:

Why wait for your flowers to grow, when you can buy them now from Linda's Flower Shop?

Or the teaser:

Why wait 6 weeks? Linda's Flower Shop.

Alternatively:

You can plant, water, weed and tend these for 8 weeks or you can let someone else do it for you. Treat yourself to flowers from Linda's Flower Shop

57. GROW YOUR OWN

If the size of your business allows it, approach a seed manufacturer and ask them to print their packaging with your business name and address on the packet. This way you are advertising their product at the same time as you are advertising your own.

Smaller florists could print their own labels and stick them onto the seed packet. Ensure labelling is clear and well laid out, like your signs. It should be linked to all your other promotional material by color, lettering style, and design.

Whether you distribute your flyer/free gift by handing it out to pedestrians or via a letterbox drop, this is a sure fire way to ensure that your flyer and your business name do not simply become part of a flyer collection, filed underneath a jar of cookies in the kitchen or discarded along with all the other unwanted bits of paper that households accumulate.

It is a rare person who will throw out a packet of seeds. The packet will remain on the kitchen bench top /desk/ refrigerator door for later use or to be passed on to someone else who might appreciate the seeds. In the interim, your business name is out there.

58. DO YOU HAVE A CARD?

The business card can be one of your greatest marketing tools or it can be one of your greatest marketing wastes. The difference is how you put it together.

When designing your business card, highlight a slogan, mission statement or catch-phrase that sets your business apart from your competitors.

You need to give your card impact and visual appeal, to gain the customer's attention. Why?

A customer wants to telephone you, so they will need to thumb through a pile of small rectangular pieces of cardboard collected from almost every business establishment or service they have ever used. Do whatever it takes to stand out from this pile of cards.

Make sure your card does not look like everyone else's. If the business card looks good, different or special, it will earn a place on the refrigerator door. If it looks like just another business card, it will be filed in the drawer along with all the other business cards, or in the garbage.

A different shape or size business cards add a touch of the unusual. They also stand out from the pile of small rectangular pieces of cardboard. You can make your card square or triangular!

59. GIVE ME A SIGN

Your business card acts as a tiny sign. Be sure it catches the potential customer's attention and clearly explains the product or service you offer.

Your business card is sometimes the first contact potential clients have with your business, so make sure it is attractive, simple, and representative of what you specialize in.

60. MORE INFORMATION PLEASE

Extra information can be printed on the back of the card. There is very little cost involved in adding further information on the back of the business card.

List your specialties, your services or your hours. List anything that will help sell your business and broaden your number of enquiries. But do not overload the card. Keep to your most important selling points while leaving the overall design simple and eye catching.

61. CALLING CARD

If you decide to door knock to improve your business, you will need to leave a card. Or maybe a "Sorry I Missed You" note would be better. Mention on the back when you will next be in the area, and make sure you do go back on the specified day.

But why leave a small rectangular business card when you can leave something more interesting?

Your business card could be cut into an even more interesting shape a flower, perhaps.

Maybe you could use a tag similar to the "Do Not Disturb" sign hung on hotel doorknobs, but with the words printed on it saying "Sorry I Missed You". And of course the name of your business, your address and telephone number appearing on the bottom.

62. FRIDGE MAGNETS

Why not make your calling card and/or business card a fridge magnet. You could combine all of the above concepts and design a "Do Not Disturb/ Sorry I Missed You" tag in the shape of a bunch of flowers, complete with a magnet on the back so it can readily be stuck on the refrigerator!

63. BE DIRECT

Direct mail is a very efficient way to get your message out to prospective clients. That is if you can get people to read it!

So how do you get your direct mail read? Make it stand out!

Think about the amount of unsolicited mail you receive at home. If something stands out by setting itself apart from other mail in the box, it will get opened. It is that old curiosity factor.

What makes someone open an envelope? People are more likely to open your envelope if it looks like a bill; if there is a hand written message on the outside; or if the outside teaser headline says that there is a free sample inside (e.g. a seed packet).

A plain white envelope can be effective. If it looks as if it has been dropped into the mailbox without a stamp, the receiver may think it is an invitation to a party rather than advertising material.

Other tips to get your direct mail read:
- Keep it fresh and do not bombard people with only one message. If they are initially interested, they might change their mind if you send the same flyer over and over again.
- Design a postcard style mail out.
- Simplicity is the key. The simplest designs can be the most effective.
- Be aware of postal restrictions. These may limit the size, shape

and style of posted material. It is best to ask at your post office before you have anything printed!
- The message and envelope must be creative and have a focus. The envelope is part of the message in direct mail.

Direct mail is not cheap, but it is an investment in the long term profitability of your business.

64. MAKING HEADLINES

Q. What is the first thing you read when you open a direct mail letter?
A. The headline.

If the headline does not catch the reader's attention and entice them to continue reading, then you have wasted your money. Do not waste your advertising dollar by discouraging your potential buyer from reading your material.

John Caples, one of the most effective copywriters of all time, has this to say: "in most advertisements, no matter how striking the illustration, the headlines are critically important. The majority of the public reads little else when deciding whether or not they are interested".[4]

And advertising guru Don Belding, in an article in a trade magazine, writes that "inquiry returns show that the headline is 50% to 75% of the advertisement". He says that selling punch in your headline is about the most important thing. It competes with news and articles and other headlines in picking out readers. Your single head line, in the average big town newspaper, competes with 350 news stories, 21 feature articles and 85 advertisements. And it competes in time, because, seen for a second, it is either heeded or passed up, and there is no return by readers'.

So tantalize the reader. Spell out the benefits of your business. Offer them something that you can give them. Some people read only the headlines. If they are pressed for time, the headline that offers the client something for nothing will entice them to read further. For example:

"FREE VASE WITH EVERY BUNCH OF FLOWERS"

65. SELL BENEFITS

Sell value and benefits, not price. Customers are looking for good value and great benefits. But remember, value is not what you say it is; it is what the customer wants.

66. MARKETING WITH THE INVOICE

A cost efficient way to market your florist is to make all your paperwork multipurpose. What better combination is there than advertising your services on your invoice?

Invoices are not usually thrown away quickly, and some people never toss them out. Whenever your customer needs to know your phone number, or what your hours are or what exactly you offer, they will easily be able to find out the answers by looking at your invoice.

Use your invoice to value add your services:

- Mention on your invoice if you deliver interstate.
- Mention if specialize in exotic or traditional flowers.
- Mention you stock vases, picture frames and/or home wares.
- Mention gift certificates.

Whatever it is you do, print it on the invoice.

Once the client has your invoice, it will be studied now and the seeds will be planted for different future purchases. You may find your business growing because people know that you offer a broad base. And when someone asks them "Do you know a good florist for my daughter's wedding?" the name of your business will be on their lips.

67. READ ALL ABOUT IT

Newsletters are a great way to keep in touch with your customers. They offer information about your store and upcoming promotions, but are presented in a soft sell style, couched in entertaining and informative stories.

Offer a newsletter or mini magazine that is distributed quarterly, revolving around the four seasons using the following ideas:

- Each season could offer information on the flowers available at that time of year.
- Sell summer and spring by cashing in on the outdoor entertainment season.
- Sell autumn and winter by discussing the lack of color in the garden at these times of year the dearth of home grown flowers to cut and bring indoors.
- Mention any promotions you have on offer for traditional flower giving seasons, such as Mother's Day, that fall into that quarter.
- Include articles that discuss the benefits of flower arrangements from the perspective of decor, style and ambience.
- Articles may contain a few thoughts on the feeling of wellbeing induced by the beauty of flowers.
- Stories could outline the benefits of scent and color to the human brain. Research on the web or do some reading in your local library.

Newsletters are also a great place to develop your customers' knowledge of the language of flowers. For example, nothing spells Christmas like mistletoe, but did you know that mistletoe the state flower of Oklahoma has been used medicinally for countless generations?

Search the internet or look in your local library for a book on the language and love of flowers, and enliven your promotional material with snippets of tradition and folk wisdom?

Your newsletter should consist of magazine style articles or key features that relate to flowers, in any way you can. Make sure the newsletter is informative and chatty, avoiding a hard sell approach. You do not want your potential customers to recognize an aggressive selling tone in your newsletter. Your customer will detect it straight away, and throw the newsletter out (Or delete it from their inbox.)

Decide whether you will distribute the newsletter by letterbox drop or by posting to mailboxes. You can also distribute the newsletter by email. Posting direct, using customers' names and addresses, would be the better choice, but you will need a database.

Once you have your newsletter ready, send it to the households in your immediate vicinity. Also mail it to local business houses which would benefit from having an account with you.

The more you can vary your marketing strategies, the more response you will get. Think of each style as an angle to a different audience and you will be on your way to making more profit for your business.

68. NO BORES!

You want people to read your newsletters, so do not make them boring! It is important when writing newsletters to include human interest items and pictures, as well as the industry news.

69. ADDRESS ME

Keep an address book on file of customers' names and addresses. You can then personalise your advertising, and keep your current customers loyal.

70. GETTING TO KNOW YOU

Take the advantage of individually getting to know your customers; try to get to know what your customers want and need from business, then tailor your newsletters to suit them.

71. THE PERSONAL TOUCH

Personalising your communication with current and prospective customers substantially increase the response you get, without increasing your costs.

In the world of emails, a personal letter to your clients is a wonderful way to market your florist. This is not direct mail. There is a difference. The direct mail letter is a generic letter that is posted to everyone and begins "Dear Customer". The personal letter mentions specific things that relate to that person alone, just as you would write a letter to a friend.

To be most effective, you can follow up the personal letter with another, detailing promotions. This has the advantage of breaking the ice, opening the door to further business. Avoid going directly to the hard sell, however refer to your previous letter.

The aim is to do the following:
- Gain the customer's attention first.
- Interest the reader with offers and benefits.
- Make reference to promotions that may be coming up.

- Put both the desire and the need to buy into the reader's mind.
- Tell the customer what they should do next: for example "Bring this letter in to Mary's Flowers before Monday the 31st to receive $10 off your next purchase of gorgeous gerberas".

At all costs avoid making the letter look like a mass produced letter. The following list of tips will ensure your letter does not look like a mass produced letter:

- use the customer's name,
- add personal pieces of information that relate specifically to that particular customer,
- sign the letter yourself,
- include a hand written "PS" to personalise the letter even further, and
- use a warm tone, as you would to a friend, and
- hand write the address on the envelope.

Big businesses are unable to market themselves in this way, as it would be cost inefficient for them. Make this your small business advantage. Customers will respond to the personal touch every time.

72. STAY IN TOUCH

It is beneficial to establish relationships with customers through the entire year. Most customers will spend their Christmas gift dollars with the retailers they have established relationships with earlier in the year.

Another reason to keep in touch with the people your promotion attracted: they might tell their friends about you. Word of mouth advertising!

73. THANK YOU

Send a hand written thank you note to your special/big customers.

74. TEXT ME

When someone orders flowers, text them once their delivery has been made. You can add an extra level of service and make sure your customers are happy.

75. POST DELIVERY SURVEY

Asking your customers for their opinion after they have placed an order is a good way to ensure high quality service. Send out a short survey the day after their flowers were delivered to get their feedback. It is also a good opportunity to include details of upcoming promotions.

CHAPTER SUMMARY

This chapter covered ways to promote your business and get your name out there. It discussed the following topics:

- Who to market to
- How to market using flyers, newsletters and business cards
- How to market using your invoice

- How to personalize your marketing
- How to stand out from your competitors.

End of chapter four (4).

5 MORE SALES, LESS BUDGET
Guerrilla marketing tactics

You may have employed many of the activities outlined in the previous chapter but your budget is running low. You would like some low-cost promotions to raise customer awareness of your business, generate more sales, and (hopefully!) increase customer loyalty.

Now it is time to release your inner guerrilla, guerrilla marketing that is!

Guerrilla marketing is when you use low cost, unconventional attention grabbing ways to draw attention to your business and products. It will help your business standout in the marketplace.

In this chapter you will find hints, tips and tricks on the following guerrilla marketing tactics:

- Corner the hard to buy for market
- Gain celebrity status
- How to get edgy
- Find homes for you flowers
- Adopt an odd slant
- And many more promotions ideas.

Release your guerrilla now!

76. GIFTS FROM THE HEART

People like to know that you have put effort into choosing a gift. But searching for the perfect present is sometimes difficult. Help your customers out. Offer them "Gifts from the Heart".

Create a new service where you suggest that your customers bring in mementos to be incorporated in the floral arrangement. A lovely personal idea is to combine flowers with a photograph. Source a wholesaler who can supply you with a range of inexpensive frames for your customer to select from.

Find:
- hearts for lovers and family members ,
- antique and contemporary styles,"
- some cute frames, aimed at the newborn/toddler market.

Other mementos that could become part of the gift of flowers could be the old teddy bear; items which signify their jobs or their hobbies; bits and pieces from childhood; books; quirky things that might spark off memories and create a laugh.

This collage approach converts a gift of the moment- fresh flowers - into something that can be kept forever. Once again you are individualizing your business, offering an additional service, and building a rapport with your clients. These are the things that will make your customers return to me.

77. GET EDGEY

Personalising the products to suit your customers' needs will give you an edge over your competitors (especially the larger supermarket flower retailers), and help you build a loyal customer base.

78. A NEW CAR!

Have you ever bought a new car and received a complimentary hamper filled with delicatessen items and a bottle of wine or champagne? Why not add a bunch of flowers? Partner with a car dealership so you can readily supply them.

And do not just think of new cars. Second hand dealers might want an idea to market their own business a gimmick to make them stand out from the crowd.

Car detailers might like to add a personal touch or a gimmick for their trade as well. They could leave behind one of your flowers in each car as a reminder of their service. This type of gimmick can become a trademark, a most powerful marketing tool.

Approach these businesses and sell the concept to them. Anything that boosts their image is bound to be met with a positive response. While promoting their business, you are selling flowers and perhaps gaining access to a few extra databases at the same time.

79. KIDS BUY FLOWERS TOO

There are hordes of school aged children out there. There are lots of schools, drama clubs, student bands and orchestras, dancing institutions, sporting groups, craft classes and the like, all of which have end of year concerts or awards nights.

And how are the teachers who tirelessly gave of themselves so that their students might enjoy their 15 minutes of fame- thanked? By being presented with a bouquet of flowers, of course!

Take hold of this opportunity and run with it. Contact every educational facility in your area.

Ask to speak to the teachers who organize the individual concerts, musicals, awards night s, and make an informal sales pitch promoting your business.

Follow the phone call up with a letter, outlining more specifically what you can offer and a broad idea of prices. Suggest that they might like to pass the information on to the student representatives from each year level.

Stay in touch with events in the school calendar and make contact with those teachers again, closer to the occasion.

Contact every cultural school art, music, dance, drama and take all the steps mentioned above. Contact every sporting group and follow the same procedure.

As every student, parent, teacher and coach knows, the end of the year or the end of the season becomes very busy. This is when the customer is more likely to contact a business owner they have already met or have a relationship with. If you provide good service they will always call on you again. This means your promotional efforts keep on working for you, again and again. The secret ingredient is the personal touch.

And remember, teachers have friends and family to buy flowers for too, and so do their friends and family!

80. REJECT ME NOT

Do not be afraid of rejection. Customers are afraid too. The customer's pulse rate actually speeds up at the end of a sale from anxiety about having made a bad buying decision.

81. ADOPT AN ODD SLANT

You are a florist. You have your own store. But there are many florists in your town; even more in your region. You are all competing for the same portion of the buying public.

- How can you attract more customers?
- You need to persuade the previously non-buying public to buy.
- You need to poach customers from other establishments.
- You need to hold on to the customers you already have.

How? Offer them something new; something different, something that no one else does. Think laterally. Adopt an unusual slant.

Choose a current fad, fashion or movement and list all the associated topics. Can you incorporate them in your current business? Can you add a complementary arm to your core trade? For example:

- Select a movement: new age.
- Choose an associated topic: astrology.
- Now relate it to your business: flowers.

Ideas: flowers associated with star signs. Colors associated with star signs, link these colors with flowers, as follows:

- Aquarius: flower, orchid; color, blue, violet.

- Libra: flower, rose; color: blue, soft pinks.
- Leo: flower, marigold, sunflower; color: gold, scarlet.
- Offer a service that caters for birthdays, or births of babies.
- Make bouquets especially for the astrological sign of the customer.
- Wrap the flowers in paper appropriate to the sign, or perhaps colored paper befitting the star sign. You could use paper with all the zodiac signs printed on it. Or the ribbon could be color appropriate.
- Attach a swing tag with a summary of the virtues of the sign.

82. CELEBRITY STATUS

Have you noticed how people follow the advice of so called gurus? Their experience, their history, their talent is known to everyone. They enjoy an elevated status. What can you learn from this? Elevate yourself. You may not have the paparazzi and magazine journalists hounding you or hanging on your every word, but you do have the ability to create your own celebrity status within your community. If you pretend you are famous, everyone else will believe you.

Start with the layout of your newspaper or magazine ad.

- When you place your ad in the newspaper, try pushing yourself to the forefront. Name your store after yourself. Choose a name of strength if you want to achieve this type of image. A first name followed by a surname works well. When you add "Florist" underneath, you now have clout.
- Place your name/business name on the left hand side. Underneath this, give yourself a spiel. Include any qualifications you might have. State your dedication to personal service. Add the actual services you provide. And then offer a discount as an extra motivator
- Top it all off with a photograph of yourself on the right-hand side with a current hairstyle and outfit.

And remember, keep running the ad. Readers will assume you have status. There will be no reason to think otherwise. This is exactly what happens to movie stars (and reality stars)!

83. DOOR-TO-DOOR FLORIST

Occasions: a florist's best time for business is catering for occasions. Mother's Day, Valentine's Day, weddings, anniversaries, funerals, births, graduations, Christmas. People buy flowers as an apology, to boost morale, to add cheer. Occasionally they will buy on whim because a color, a variety or the price entices them.

But how do you secure the consumers' purchasing power on a more permanent and steady basis? How can you boost sales on a nondescript day of no significant month?

Make your florist shop do twice the amount of work. Deliver flowers door-to-door. Successful vacuum cleaner corporations do it. Huge telephone companies do it. Why cannot small florists do it too?

Very few people wake up in the morning and decide "I think I'll buy a vacuum cleaner today." Yet this form of direct marketing has built a company that spans the globe, and has required no other form of advertising. Similarly, some people do not buy flowers often because they think of them as a non-essential item. But if you can offer quality, price and ease of purchase, you can help overcome this stumbling block.

The benefits are twofold: for the customer, you offer an opportunity to buy immediately; for you, there is the chance to promote and advertise your own business.

For the customer
- A smiling face at your front door, offering a handful of vibrant flowers, is visually appealing. It sends out warm, fuzzy feelings. Warm, fuzzy feelings induce people to buy.
- You are offering the customer ease of purchase. No driving. No parking. No walking. The flowers come to them.
- You are saving the customer time.
- You are inviting customer intimacy, building a bond whereby you are allowed into their home to help with the decision of variety, color, arrangement, and placement to suit the decor or mood of the room. A judiciously offered compliment on some unusual feature of their decorating will further endear you to the householder.
- This allows you to cultivate a relationship with the customer. You are seen as a helper, not just a salesperson. You are personalising the service, fine- tuning price and product to their requirements. In the eyes of the customer, you are adding excitement and anticipation to the service.
- You have the opportunity to know the people you are selling to, giving you the chance to suggest different colors or arrangements without appearing to be salesman-like or pushy. This will win customer loyalty by adding variety, preventing the concept from becoming stale and the customer from dropping the service.

For you
- You are being proactive. You are taking the decision of which florist away from the customer. You are the florist at their own front door. You are no longer one of the many florist shops on several streets in every town or city in the world.

- You are helping them establish a flower-buying habit.
- You are advertising your business while maximising the opportunity for sales.
- You are getting twice the amount of trade for the same business.

84. DELIVERY WITH A DIFFERENCE

When an unexpected parcel or special delivery arrives, it usually receives considerable attention from the recipient. We discussed direct mail in the previous chapter and how important it is your mail gets read.

Why not experiment with the method of delivery? This way your mail might deliver a greater impact. For example, get a courier to deliver the mail and the addressee having to sign for it ensures that it gets to the person you want it to reach. The costs involved with this type of direct mail are more than the traditional method of postage, but your guarantee of the mail "getting through" is greater. You can target fewer people, and those you do target are people of influence.

As a florist owner/operator you may still be thinking "How can I use this concept to give me a competitive edge?" Easy! Follow these steps:

- Draw up a list of 20-40 names of female business managers or owners in your business district who are not on your current database of customers.
- You may already know some of these people, or you can source the businesses from the local phone directory. If the manager or owner's name is not in the ad, trying ringing the business and asking for it, saying you need to address a letter to them.
- Now you need to design a letter, which will be couriered to them and deliver impact. It is recommended you use plain, high-quality paper and envelopes. The message should also tie in with a call to action, such as your monthly special.

The letter could go as follows:
Date

Ms Julia Rose (title) (company) (address)

Dear Ms Rose,

RE: SORRY

As manager of (your florist name), I am sorry to inform you that this is not a bouquet of our gorgeous gerberas to brighten up your office.

However, for the month of May we have bouquets of gerberas on special for just $30 to liven up your workplace-and your home! Delivery is also free within a 10-kilometre radius.

Do not delay any longer-treat yourself! Bring your workplace environment alive with the power of flowers.

Sincerely,
(Your name)
(Your address & details)

85. ADD IT UP

Initially you can test the effectiveness of the campaign with 20 names at a cost of $3 per letter couriered. The outlay will be $60. A redemption rate of just 30%, approximately six women, buying flowers at $30, brings $180 back. Take away the letter delivery at $60 and you have made $120 from a simple yet witty letter couriered directly to the business woman.

This type of direct mail may generate word of mouth in these women's circles of friends and associates. This is also a higher-earning market that is more likely to buy products such as flowers-for themselves or for gifts. Aiming your direct mail at this profitable market will make your initial outlay of $60 work for you over and over again.

86. CORNERING THE HARD-TO-BUY- FOR MARKET

Buying presents can be difficult, so make it easy for your customers. Offer a gift certificate.

You can offer the traditional one-off gift voucher concept. There will be a portion of your market that would buy these. Remember, though, to remind them that it is an option. Sometimes people need to buy a present, cannot think of an idea, but it is the thing that catches their eye at that particular time that wins their dollar.

Make the certificate look good. It is important not to skimp on the design of your gift certificate because the certificate is given in lieu of the gift.

People will be more tempted to buy your gift voucher if it is attractive to the eye. On opening the card, the receiver will be pleased to receive a beautiful certificate.

The certificate is another way to promote your business, so you want it to look attractive. The voucher might be shown to friends, stuck with a magnet onto the refrigerator, where others will see it, before the flowers are redeemed. And an idea for future purchase of a certificate, by the receiver herself, has been planted.

87. ONE STEP FURTHER

Now take the idea of the gift certificate one step further and appeal to a different market. Get together a package deal and sell the gift certificate (and therefore the flowers) in a different way.

- How would "Flowers for the month of May" look written in beautiful cursive script on a voucher? You could offer the potential gift buyer a special rate for four weekly deliveries of fresh bouquets to really spoil someone special.

- What about "Fresh flowers every week until Christmas"? Or
- "Three weeks' worth of flowers?"

You could devise your own length of time-offer different options, or negotiate with the customer, considering their budget.

This adds oomph to an old idea, and makes a one-off gift longer-lasting. This is attractive to the buyer, the receiver, and to you because you are prolonging the amount of time you are in contact with your client. Building up a relationship and reinforcing your business name repeatedly over a period of time. Smart advertising!

Maybe a surprise package would entice some buyers who planned to use the prolonged gift voucher. The buyer could tick the boxes appropriate to their choice of individual flowers.

Be aware that some unscrupulous individuals out there are scanning gift vouchers into their PCs and manipulating dates or recreating identical certificates. Here are some to tips to avoid this:

- Use distinctive paper, a stock not readily available.
- Hand-write at least some information on your voucher and sign it.
- Use a distinctive-colored pen.
- Keep a record of all vouchers given out-who bought them, and for whom.
- Number each voucher and tick them off when they are redeemed.

88. A NEW ANGLE

Easter: eggs, fluffy rabbits and downy chickens. Valentine's Day: satin hearts and chocolates. Tartan ribbons for Christmas and Mother's Day bouquets on Mother's day. You are rushed off your feet at these times, but between times do you find yourself saying "Business has been a bit quiet"? Or do you just accept that it is always quiet at that time of year?

Yes, there are always birthdays, anniversaries and the births of babies. But what else is there? How else can you boost your business?

The solution is to make your own occasions or find fresh angles on the existing occasions in people's lives. How about:

- The New Business Owner?
- The New Graduate?
- The New Home Owner?
- Religious occasions?
- The Thank You?

Do not give your business an opportunity to slow down. Have the steps in place ahead of time so that your alternative occasions are known about, to fill the retail gap.

In other words, forward planning is the key to profitability and long-term success. He or she who plans today is here tomorrow. Efficient managers plan all their business functions and activities in advance and avoid at all costs managing by crisis. People need to know what you offer before they are able to buy.

Have examples of your work on display and signs in the window and in the store. Remember to make use of the counter space and the area behind the counter.

Carry an array of mementos that can be added to the bouquet to personalize your gift and dress up your flowers-and add a few dollars to the customer's spending price.

Ask your local printing house about tags. Can these be cut to particular shapes to coordinate with the occasion-for example, a mortar-board for a new graduate? Now you have another decoration to individualize your bouquet.

And, of course, add a card. But make sure the cards look great.

Promote your willingness to invent new ways of presenting your work. The more you can cater to people's needs, the more they will use your service. Too often it appears to be the other way around in retail stores: buyers feel that they are being used by the retailer.

This approach will ensure that the customer returns to your store whenever they need a gift, even if it is not the traditional flower-selling season. You want them to think flowers on all kinds of occasions, all year round. This translates to more buyers, more sales-more profit.

89. BUILDING HOUSES FOR FLOWERS

Target the new house market. This time, go to the people who build the houses. Approach architects and builders and give them a bunch of business cards.

Alternatively, they could share the cost of a bouquet of flowers with you. They would then present their clients with the flowers, welcoming them to their new home. The architect or builder's name and the name of their organization would be included on the card. It is an extension of their goodwill, their name is associated with another positive message, their gift of flowers will be seen and talked about, and the receivers will mention where the flowers came from.

Of course, the name of your florist will also be on the card, and you will receive many positive business benefits. In addition, you will have another potential client in your already growing database.

90. STYLE

If you plan to supply flowers to larger businesses and companies in your community, you can make your life a lot easier by having a number of set style arrangements for your clients to choose from. You can even give them names: "the house warmer", "the romantic" and "the lavish romantic".

91. BLAZING A TRAIL

Remember Little Red Riding Hood, innocently picking flowers on the way to Grandma's house? Be the Big Bad Wolf and lure Little Red Riding Hood off her path! If you have been shopping overseas, you will have seen the spruikers in the streets who offer you the very products you need.

I am not suggesting using bad business practice, but to find a positive way of directing people to your door. Try the following guerrilla tactics to entice people to step off their normal path.

- Post teasers in the street at periodic intervals to catch people's attention and direct them to your door.
- Learn from the McDonald's signs that tell you that it is '4 km to the next McDonald's'. Try "One Block to Rebecca's Flower Shop".
- Post a thought of the day or thought of the week in your window or on the A-frame sign in front of your store. Try to place these in the street at regular intervals.
- Write a few lines of information about the flowers that are currently in season and, again, post it regularly in your display window or in the street.
- Find some quotes from well-known poets and writers who have referred to flowers in their works. Change them often. Even the Bible is full of floral references!
- Devise an ongoing comic strip that can be taped to your window. Even better if the theme of flowers can be worked into the story. Or ask a local art student to come up with something. The saga about the main character could involve romance, Valentine's Day; Mother's Day-all the traditional flower-giving occasions can be worked in. And add some others such as the dinner party guests or the house guests from hell. It is your story. This could be as serious or as funny as you like, but people will read it, no matter what. And once they know about the routine, they will come back to keep up with the latest. And they will tell all their friends about it.

92. PACKAGE DEALS

Everyone loves a package deal. It works for the tourism industry-there is no reason it will not work for you. In the tourism industry, package deals work well to lift sales in the off season. Use the same way of thinking to increase your trade during quiet times. You might like to attach the idea to a time of year, or perhaps extend the concept to a particularly quiet day or night of the week.

- Appeal to the hostess who is short of time or the worker in need of a night's pampering.

- Hook up your florist shop with a takeaway store, delicatessen, bakery, music store and wine shop close to your premises.
- Each business offers a discount to lure the customers in.
- Share the printing costs. You could even jointly produce a poster-style calendar.
- Distribute the flyers and nominate the night or week the package is available.
- Tick the box that relates to your business, date and stamp it, and get all the associated businesses in the package deal to do the same.
- Customers must have bought the goods within the agreed time frame in order to receive the discount from each store. They can choose to forgo the full package, buying from your business only or from one of the others. Be flexible.

You have still cut your printing costs and got your name out there, and you have given your business another opportunity to make a sale.

93. MORE THAN JUST A FLOWER SHOP

Some people need a little help with their gift buying. Some are looking for a gift that is "a bit different". Others, lacking creative flair, just do not know what goes with what. Some do not have the time to think about it, let alone to source and carry out the purchase. This is where you step in. Offer a flower hamper.

You will need a range of goodies and treats, such as:
- flowers
- CDs
- candles
- candle holders
- confectionery
- bath salts/oils
- body lotions
- coffee beans
- tea bags
- biscuits books
- gourmet foods.

You can add to the list as you please. Offer your customers a choice of products from the above list. Or offer hampers with set items at set prices.

Other stores tend to offer hampers only at Christmas time. Try offering your hampers all year round. Market your concept as innovative, unique and accessible. This is sure to:
- keep your regulars coming back, and
- introduce new customers to your store;

both of which will increase your sales.

94. SELLING FLOWERS TO BUSINESSES

Take your flowers to other businesses. By taking both florist products and your services to the owner or manager, you are:

- making it easy for them,
- helping them, and
- saving them time.

From a more personal perspective, you are:

- offering your expertise, knowledge and flair;
- enhancing the premises for customers, themselves and their staff;
- tailor-making arrangements according to the look of the room to create impact and style, not simply dumping a generic bunch of flowers in a vase on the counter;
- joining their side and creating warmer relations within your local business community.

Impress on the retailer that their business will improve because of the presence of your flowers. Their premises will look good, stylish, friendly, and happy. People will enjoy being there, staying there, coming back. Reiterate that relaxed, happy customers will buy. They will feel more at home, especially if the environment is otherwise clinical or intimidating. This is particularly true of women, who make the majority of purchase decisions.

For you, the florist, the benefits are many. You are increasing your exposure. Your business card is attached to your bouquet for customers to see. Your friendly face, your uniform, your decorated car are on show. You have made yourself more visual. You are promoting yourself.

The possibilities in the commercial sector are endless. Here are just a few suggestions:

- Retail stores, especially women's fashion
- Hairdressers
- Beauty therapists
- Nail technicians
- Cosmetic surgeons
- Physiotherapists
- Psychologists and counsellors
- Weight consultants and nutritionists
- Stress managers, massage therapists and naturopaths

Any establishment that appears technical, sterile, unfriendly, intimidating or scary is in dire need of an injection of the warm fuzzies. These make you feel happy. When you feel happy you feel comfortable. If you feel comfortable you will come back. So think again.

- Doctors' surgeries.
- Dental surgeries.
- Accountants' offices.
- The bank manager's desk.

95. SHARING COSTS

Most proactive business owners distribute flyers and brochures to advertise their businesses. They do this because it works. But why pay for all your advertising alone, when you can share the costs with others?

Get together with other retailers and service industries and share printing costs. You might decide to print your business on one side of the paper and your colleague's on the other. You could divide the paper horizontally, vertically or diagonally and share halves that way.

Marketing your business this way creates a win/win situation:

- Printing and distribution costs are reduced, increasing your profit.
- Because of this you might be able to advertise more often.
- You have the chance of gaining customers from your colleague's complementary business.
- The chances of your flyer being retained are greater.

Getting your business name out there + sharing printing costs while you do it = more profit!

96. WELL DONE

Everyone likes achievers. Everyone likes associating with achievers. And, as the motivational gurus say: "Surround yourself with achievers and positive people and you will become one yourself".

So scan the newspapers for individuals in your area who are on their way to success. Choose the big guys or, for an easier path to their doors, target those who have been recognized but who have not yet been thrust into the highly competitive world of marketing and sponsorship. It does not matter whether they are known for their musical achievements, their sporting prowess, their theatrical abilities or their business acumen.

Send them a congratulatory note or card praising their achievements and sign it, printing the name of your store on the bottom. Include a discount on their next purchase to entice them into your store.

97. HERB GARDEN

It is common for businesses to try to make more money by taking on the distribution of local products. With this type of concept it is important that you do not overcrowd your store. Selling unrelated products can also lower the professional image of your store.

Bearing in mind the importance of keeping your florist business in high esteem, ask yourself:

- What more can I add to my product range to entice customers into my store who would not normally enter?

- What kind of products will not involve a huge outlay of money?
- What products relate to my existing service and products?

Why not introduce the sale of herbs? Everyone would love a herb garden. These small plants are easy to maintain in store. The freshness and smell of fragrant plants will also help to create an ambience, contributing to a pleasant buying environment. And, most importantly, they are related to your core product: plants.

As an extension of this idea, you can sell also the related products. If you sold small window or planter boxes there would be no need to compete directly with the local garden center. You would instead be creating a boutique feel, small and specialized. Boutique = luxury = flowers.

Diversifying your product range is an excellent way of enhancing the purchase transaction from your current customer base, and of increasing traffic flow. There is something more for them to buy when they enter your store or when they reach the counter. And there is potential for more profit for your store.

98. CARD GAMES

OK, so you have designed some super special business cards that are eye-catching, specific, clear and effective.

They have your business name, specialty service, address, e-mail address, web address and phone number. Now what to do with them?

Spread them!

Business cards are your little business advertisements, and you want to spread them around to get noticed. Talk to libraries, supermarkets, office blocks, businesses campuses etc.-in fact, anywhere there are people!

Ask at hospitals, dentists' and doctors' offices too. Ask whether you may post your cards on their notice boards, in their bathrooms, or in other areas where they will be seen. Be creative: anywhere is good as long as your prospective clients can see it.

Pass out

Your business cards are no good to you while you are holding onto them. Do not pass up any opportunity to hand out your cards to other people.

Did you buy petrol this morning? Leave your card. Did you go to the shops to buy groceries? How many cards did you leave, either with individuals or on the counter? Did you just happen to be carrying a gorgeous bunch of flowers? Did you talk to anyone?

Drop your card on the shelf in the health food section of the supermarket. If people are shopping in that section for grits and gruel, vitamins and health supplements, the odds are that they will be interested in your services as well. You have got to be always thinking along these lines and looking for opportunities to promote yourself.

If you do not think the people shopping in your area are interested in your services, then shop where your clients do. Infiltrate your target market and get to know their habits and preferences.

Paid any local bills by mail lately? Did you include your business card in the envelope? Perhaps the person opening the mail will need your service or know of a friend who does. Do not waste an opportunity to get known, as every encounter has the potential to generate more profit for you.

99. SOMETHING FOR NOTHING

You have heard how valuable word-of-mouth referral is. The problem is that not all clients will run around the local neighborhood voluntarily, raving about your florist, no matter how good you and your staff are. The simple reasons for this are: they were never asked; or the idea did not even occur to them.

You can overcome these short-term impediments by actually asking your satisfied clients whether they would mind providing you with a testimonial. Be sure to explain to them carefully how and where their testimonial will be used.

You may simply want to write their quotation on a sheet of butcher's paper and post it in a window. Or you might want to carry the idea through to flyers, letters or even into the mainstream media.

Most people will be delighted to have their comments published. You could even change the testimonial so regularly that it becomes a marketing gimmick. It could take on the same tone as a soap opera, where the locals tune in to see who has been to your business lately and to find out what the latest one has said. This can add a bit of fun to the process and takes the heat off one or two clients, making them more likely to agree to participate. You could even find it takes on a life of its own, as competitive nature kicks in, with some individuals clamoring for their 15 minutes of fame!

Even those who say no will be flattered that you asked them anyhow. Often they will come around with a little gentle persuasion; if not, they will enjoy telling their friends the story. And that is more publicity for you.

There is now a group of satisfied customers who are happy to say nice things about your business and its staff. It is free, and it is good for your business.

It is important that you do not pay for testimonials or for their subsequent use. The whole point is people voluntarily recommending your business, without being paid. They are going to do it for nothing because it is flattering to them, because it is the truth, and because they know that every time they return for an appointment you and your staff are going to give them extra special care and attention.

100. WORD OF MOUTH

Customers can become your cheapest and most effective form of advertising. Treat them well and your business will benefit from their positive word of mouth.

101. LAUGH YOUR WAY TO MORE PROFIT

Creativity and humor go hand in hand. An injection of humor could well see your sales increasing.

Humor has a feeling of rawness, of honesty. And honesty is a virtue that every merchant wants to promote in relation to their business. Honesty wins customers' confidence. Honesty sells.

Humor can be used in your business in many ways. For example:

- your uniform
- your car
- your happy-go-lucky manner
- your mail outs
- your newspaper ads.

102. ADVERTISING WHILE GETTING THERE

You are in the business of selling. If you want to optimize your profits, why limit yourself to the usual business hours? Create opportunities to sell your business 24 hours a day.

One idea is to use your car to advertise. You drive to your door-to-door customers. You drive to your restaurateur customers. You drive to your retail/business/service customers. While you drive, advertise.

Think pizza-delivery vehicles-the ones with the pizza box on the roof. Apply the same principle to your florist business with the following tips:

Paint flowers on your car and add the name of the company. Construct a sunflower and attach it. Play your own jingle over a speaker. Be creative.

Magnetic labels that attach to the door of your car can be printed with your name, logo, address, phone number. (But beware-these can become collector's items!)

A sign writer can adhere vinyl-cut lettering to your car. The lettering can be easily removed when you want it to go.

103. CREATE A MOOD

Consumers these days are more aware than ever of their environment and are taking a critical view of their surroundings. The recent popularity of Feng Shui has highlighted how important it is to place furniture and products in specific areas for the most positive effect. The home and business environment is both created and greatly affected by what is in that space.

Here is how you take advantage of this trend. Your core products, flowers, play a large part in creating mood and atmosphere.

Some consumers will have a limited knowledge of what flowers represent, in particular roses. They may know, for example, that red roses signify passionate love, but are they aware that yellow roses mean jealousy? There is a brief appendix at the end of this book with some examples of traditional flower meanings.

You can take this concept one step further and use it to enhance your in-store flower displays. For each bucket of flowers make up a medium-sized placard with a thin wooden stem attached to place in the bucket with the flowers. You should have a separate placard for each type of flower. On the placard write the flower type and what it can do for the consumer's environment.

For example, your placards may read:

Orchids - Create a sense of freedom and space in the home.

Water lilies - Ancient Japanese tradition says they create wealth for the home.

Researching at your local library or on the internet is a great way of gaining information on the meanings of flowers. As a florist you should know what your flowers can do for the home or business environment.

104. CAUSING PROFIT

Being involved with non-profit organizations can promote your florist business to a higher standing in the community. Not only does it give your business a better rapport with the community, it can spark interest and business from customers and potential customers alike.

The AIDS ribbons, Red Nose day and Jeans for Genes day have been much-publicized events which many small to large businesses have backed. And they have received publicity in return. In marketing terms, this is called cause-related marketing.

The cause can be anything that you feel relates to your area and that you feel your community will support. It can be something as simple as helping to put in a new garden at the local senior citizens' home. To fund the cause you might donate $1 from every bunch of gerberas sold on Fridays, or $1 from every bouquet of flowers worth over $50. You might even use the donation method to help successfully introduce a new product line. How you structure the promotion is entirely up to you.

It is important to produce promotional material that will support the cause in flyers or by displaying a banner outside your store. Make your exercise extremely visible and you will soon find it becomes a talking point in your community.

105. MARRYING YOUR BUSINESS

It is no news to florists that the wedding industry is huge. But do not just sit back and wait for the bride to come to you to order the bridal bouquet. The following suggestions will make sure the bride cannot possibly miss you.

Meet the proprietors of all the local wedding related businesses. Get together a bunch of flowers and a pile of business cards and display your creativity on their counters and in their windows. Hook up with:

- a bridal shop
- suit hire and wedding hire outlets

- car hire companies
- cake decorators
- photographers
- restaurateurs and wedding reception venues
- stationery stores
- luxury fabric stores
- hairdressers
- beauticians
- wedding organizers.

Read the classified advertisements in your local newspapers and make a list of all the newly engaged couples. You can send them a personal letter of congratulations while also offering your unique floral services.

Get your business mentioned in the usual bridal promotion in the newspaper.

Do not forget about the bride and groom after the wedding. No doubt their special day was a huge success, and your flowers contributed to the occasion.

- Send them a personal letter wishing them well, commenting on their fine taste in floral arrangements. Avoid the hard sell but offer your future services.
- Remember, the newlywed couple will enjoy making a home. You hope that part of that nesting instinct will include improving the decor with flowers.
- They might require flowers to decorate the table while entertaining guests.
- They will require flowers for Mother's Day, birthdays, anniversaries, Valentine's Day, friendships, to say thank you, the births of babies.
- Remember, these people also have friends and relatives.

You will build a solid base for your business by offering good service to the happy couple. So plant your seeds and watch them grow into more profit.

106. NETWORKING

Think about all the opportunities that exist with clubs. Get a brainstorming session going with your staff/associates, and jot down all of the clubs/associations/meeting places/ committees/ church groups where you can make contact with groups of people.

Do not forget to access the Yellow Pages, the Internet and your local library for publications and listings of clubs and associations in your locality. At the completion of this exercise, you should have a very long list to work from, so choose a particular category and get started.

Sporting clubs are one obvious starting place, and there are two categories within this grouping:

a) clubs where people are active participants in the sport; and

b) clubs where people are: spectators, administrators, coaches, assistants.

You can market your business to each of these clubs.

1. Clubs where people are active participants in the sport, such as netball, baseball, volleyball, basketball, dance, golf, tennis, football, racquet ball, bowling and gymnasiums. In this instance you might approach the committee/coach/team captain and offer a substantial discount to all team/committee/coaching members and their families who attend your florist. You might even be able to broker a deal that gets you some free advertising in the club newsletter in exchange for that discount.

2. Clubs where people are spectators/administrators/ coaches/assistants because of the involvement of their children, such as little league, scouting and junior swimming.

107. BRAINSTORMING

To encourage open and creative thinking, try brainstorming with a diverse group of people rather than likeminded people. You try it at your next dinner party. This will result in broader and more innovative promotional ideas.

When brainstorming creative design ideas bury your preconceptions about limitations. The objective is to open your mind and list as many ideas as possible without stifling creativity.

Brainstorming is time think outside the square. Take out a paper and pad and start thinking about all the places you could sell your flowers; apart from inside your own flower shop.

Retail outlets and business receptions

- retail outlets: boutiques, shoe shops, furniture, lighting;
- service industries: restaurants, hotels, motels, hairdressers, beauty salons, interior decorators;
- professional offices: doctors, dentists, counsellors;
- sales professionals: real estate agents, car dealers.

Gift format

- certificates
- hampers
- packages.

Welcome format

- real estate agents for new home buyers
- car dealers for new car owners
- new business owners.

Thanking clients

- thank them for their support during the year.

Events, awards, promotions
- race days
- sporting events, awards evenings
- school events, graduation evenings, concerts
- little theatre, light opera societies, dance studios, drama club evenings
- modelling schools

Door to door

Homes businesses

Community groups
- mother's groups, child care centers, kindergartens
- senior citizen groups.

In short, think of every opportunity you possibly can to sell flowers in every format imaginable. The broader your retail base, the more solid your business will be. This means you will make more money and your business will be around for a lot longer.

108. STAFF THINKING

Encourage and reward open and creative thinking from your staff. Not only will you get a greater range of ideas, but the staff will feel as though their opinions are valued, enhancing job satisfaction and reducing voluntary turnover.

109. THE NOTEBOOK

Always be on the lookout for new, impressive ideas you could adapt to your business. Keep a notebook with you, to jot down the ideas as soon as you spot them. When it comes time for brain storming promotional ideas, refer to your notebook.

CHAPTER SUMMARY

This chapter discussed how to release your inner guerrilla, guerrilla marketing that is! It covered the following guerrilla marketing strategies:
- Corner the hard to buy for market
- Gain celebrity status
- How to get edgy
- Find homes for you flowers
- Adopt an odd slant
- And many more promotions ideas

End of chapter five (5).

6 SMALL COST, BIG IMPACT
Get noticed on a small budget

OK. So you have done the newspaper ads, the posters in the windows, the A-frame at the front of your shop, the business card. You know you need to drum up more attention, but the cost of more advertising seems out of your league. Do not let that stop you!

Getting noticed does not take a big budget. You do need to be creative and available, to realize the opportunities that are out there.

In this chapter you will find hints, tips and tricks on the following low cost ways to promote your business:

- Making your mark
- Make the most of early morning traffic
- Winners are grinners
- Finding houses for your flowers
- Business arrangements
- Joining forces with other businesses
- Goodwill, frequent buyers and VIPs
- And many more.

Start getting noticed now!

110. MAKING YOUR MARK

You want a flyer that will be kept, not thrown out with the garbage. You want a memento that will not cost the earth. How about a bookmark?

You can hand bookmarks to your customers at the end of their transaction. Hand them out as you would a flyer, or include them in direct mail outs.

Design your own, adopt the ideas of a graphic artist, or combine the two perspectives, then take the artwork to your local printer. The basics are a rectangular piece of cardboard and a hole punched in one end with a ribbon threaded through and knotted. Tell the designer and printer your budgetary requirements, because the type of card and its thickness, the number of colors used, the style of the design and metallic paint will all influence the cost.

For an effective marketing campaign, the layout and color scheme should be consistent with the colors of your logo. If your budget allows it, your printer will also print the name of your store on the ribbon itself. Your job is simply to cut the ribbon into lengths and thread it through the hole.

What you put on the bookmark should be consistent with the image of your business. For example, a business catering for the top end of the market would need a more stylish look. But if you are directing your business at a more suburban family sector or at older people you could alienate potential clients if you use this polished, up-market look. Your customers may respond better to something homey and familiar.

An extra reason for clients to keep the bookmark could be the inclusion of information consistent with your business. For example, list flowers and their meanings. Mention saleable flowers that go with dates of birth, or wedding anniversaries. Include tips on how to keep flowers fresher for longer-anything you can think of that would be of interest to the flower buyer.

Another idea is to print a series of different tips which can encourage customers to collect and keep your bookmarks. Or you could continually update the tips, once each batch is disseminated. Of course your business name, address and phone number will be prominent. You might like also to include your opening hours, the services you provide, and any extra products you sell.

111. HAPPY BIRTHDAY

As children, we all looked forward to our birthdays. Not only were we a year older but, more importantly in our eyes, we looked forward to the presents. As adults, we still become a year older with each birthday, but the deluge of presents has usually dropped off dramatically.

How can you, the florist, rectify this situation? Make your regular customers feel special again, and offer them a gift from your store.

Use your database to access your customers' birthdays. They may not want to give away their year of birth and that is ok. You only need the day and month. Send them a birthday card and include a certificate offering a discount on their next purchase.

Make a fuss of the customer when they enter the store, and ask about their birthday celebrations. You might even like to keep a stash of wrapped fruitcake on hand, and give them a slice after the transaction has been made.

The benefits of this type of promotion are numerous:

- You are sending out flyers to promote your business and to remind your customers to return to your store.
- This is not perceived as random advertising, which some customers might tend to ignore. You have targeted a specific customer, with a good reason to send out the flyer in the first place.
- The customer will be pleased to be remembered by you, lifting their perception of both you and the store itself.
- They will return to your store to receive their discount and perhaps find something else to buy.
- The customer will be thrilled with the idea and will hopefully tell all their friends.

Personal attention is one of the most effective ways to retain your customers and win new ones. Many stores nowadays concentrate heavily on moving stock and increasing turnover, regarding customers as walking dollar signs. If you can show your customers you are thinking about them at a personal level, they will return to lap up the attention.

Everyone likes to feel special!

112. FAMILY DEALS

When you have secured one member of the family as a customer, it makes good marketing sense to target other family members. Tell each of your current clients that you offer a family deal. Print a card that lists all their family members who live in your area. If there are more than, say, three (or choose a number you prefer), offer them a 10% discount (again, your choice of discount).

In your database you will need to list their names, addresses and phone numbers. Use the database to contact them directly when you are experiencing a slow week or when you need a little extra cash. Offer them 15% off if they buy their flowers within a given time frame.

Maybe you could make up a fun promotion, like Sisters' Day. Allocate your own day of the year then run a promotional campaign announcing your fabricated selling occasion. Again it would make sense to choose a time of year that is otherwise slow. The rules are that both family members (sisters) need to attend on the given day for both to receive a discount. Ask the sisters to fill out a form giving their addresses and phone numbers and keep them on your database. Now keep in touch with them for marketing purposes.

Mother's Day is a good day to promote your services. And you could add a twist to the occasion: when the son or daughter buys a bunch of flowers for their parent, they receive a discount on a bunch for themselves.

The purpose behind these ideas is to extend your customer base and to catch more sales. In the process, you are generating more publicity for your business. Any positive publicity you can dream up that will make your business more secure and stable is bound to make you more profit.

113. JOINING FORCES

What one thing common to people the world over makes them smile and sends a little tingling sensation through their body? Getting something for free!

"But how can I give away stuff from my store?" you ask, "I'll go broke!" The solution is easy. You give away stuff from other people's stores.

Think about cross-promotional opportunities with colleagues in complementary businesses. What kinds of business would like to associate with a florist? The list could be very long. Here are a few: restaurants, fashion stores, wine stores, chocolate shops, lingerie stores, home ware stores, linen houses, catering companies.

Would the chocolate shop owner be prepared to offer your clients a two for the price of one deal if you directed 100 or so customers to their establishment? Would they be interested in offering their chocolate loving patrons a discount on flowers at your establishment?

Think of photographers. Would they offer a discount price on the cost of a sitting? Would a house cleaning company offer a discount on a service or include a small, cheerful bunch of flowers as a memento of their spring-cleaning deal?

If your business is located in a shopping complex, try to make friends with retailers in neighboring shops. You can exchange promotional ideas and create complementary advertising campaigns.

114. EARLY-MORNING TRAFFIC

Mornings are often a crazy time for people racing to get to work. Promotionally, this is an excellent time to target people, but not with boring flyers. Try something a bit out of the ordinary.

Why not give a flower to each female passer-by to brighten up their day?

Have a staff member in clearly identifiable uniform (even a screen-printed T-shirt will do) handing out single blooms. The flower you choose will obviously depend on the season, what is available and most economical. Ideally you will be able to bulk-buy long-stemmed flowers whatever the season.

The figures for a promotion aimed at 400 women are as follows:

Buying 400 flowers at .50c equals a payout of $200.

A 3% redemption rate means 12 people buying bouquets of flowers for, say, $50.

Your sales income is $600 - you have paid the outlay three times over.

Handing out a flower is more than advertising. It is a gift and a sample of your products. Attach a small card to the flower, saying something along the lines of:

Do not just wake up and smell the coffee, take time out to smell the flowers!!

(Name of Florist and address)

Your staff member can select women who look like potentially valuable customers of your store-for example, with an upmarket boutique florist, those who are particularly well dressed.

Women are more likely to go back to their offices and job sites and talk about their find. Many love to chat and show off something that not everybody in the office has. If the small tag attached is quirky, there is more chance they will talk about it, feel special and spread the word further-thus creating more free advertising for you.

115. FINDING HOUSES FOR YOUR FLOWERS

Go direct to the people whose business is houses-real estate agents. Furnish their counter with examples of your flowers and leave some business cards.

Take the idea one step further. Imagine all the new home owners who would love to receive a small bunch of flowers- a gift "For the New Home Owner". The real estate agent could share the costs with you-after all, their name and organization will be included on the card. This means they look good, their name is once again out there, and no longer do they appear to be the salesman you never see again once the sale has been made.

But your name is also on the card. You too will receive the positive business benefits.

Another spin on this idea is to sell to the house vendor the concept of buying flowers from your florist shop. For open house days, real estate agents will switch on lamps, play music, bake cakes and brew coffee-all to produce that special ambience that encourages a sale. Why not add flowers to the list?

A beautiful arrangement of flowers on the hall table near the entry, on the dining table, in the kitchen or bathroom will enhance any house. Flowers work particularly well to lift a dead or dull spot.

116. FLOWERS TO RESTAURATEURS

Restaurants. Food. Wine. Conviviality. Friends. Romance. Fun. Flowers. Have you noticed how many restaurants do not have fresh flowers on their tables? Have you ever wondered why? Is it the time required to buy them? Is it the effort required to look after them? Is it the cost? Do they know which variety to buy? Do they understand the look they want to achieve?

Take your expertise to the restaurateurs and attack their uncertainties and negative attitudes head on. You can offer a daily service. But be prepared to negotiate with your client. Together you may decide to service the flowers every two or three days. Work out a schedule together, taking into account the lifespan of the flowers and the cost-effectiveness, for both you and the client.

With a larger order you might offer free vases as part of the contract price. This will appeal to the client, because they feel they are getting something for nothing. It also removes the task of needing to buy the vases themselves, and it gives you creative input into the overall appearance of the arrangement.

117. A BUSINESS ARRANGEMENT

If you plan to supply flowers direct to business establishments, it can be helpful to provide them with a portfolio of numbered arrangements. This way the customer can simply quote a number over the phone representing the type of arrangement they want.

118. A FLOWER FOR ALL SEASONS

Take a tip from the retail clothing industry: try a seasonal angle on selling flowers. About three weeks before the change of seasons, start your promo based around the impending season.

Spring is obvious. You could use the theme of spring cleaning, starting afresh, or chasing winter away. Name the flowers in season. Offer a discount. Give people a reason to come into your store.

Summer is a good target. Refer the customer to the entertainment season, to outdoor barbecues. Mention the flowers in season again, and offer a discount.

Autumn can be treated the same way, but play on the need to cozy up the house this time, to highlight the movement away from summer and to encourage more buying according to the season.

The *winter* angle would be to chase away the dreary days by brightening up your home with a fabulous bunch of flowers.

Make up some packages within the seasons to encourage flower buying throughout the year. For example, if customers buy two bunches of seasonal flowers during the first two weeks of May, they will receive a discount on the third and fourth bunch.

119. MORE HOMES FOR YOUR FLOWERS

Keep taking your wares into other shops. Let the customers from those shops know who you are.

Bookstores

People who buy books are apt to appreciate the finer things in life. So just behind the counter of a bookshop is a good place to show your skills as a florist. Placing your business cards on the counter is a handy way to advertise who and where you are.

You could carry a few specialized books in your store as a return favor. Place them around the store to create landscapes in your display arrangements, simulating a corner in the home or office environment.

Purchase of a package of books could earn customers a discount on your flowers or perhaps a free bunch. Negotiate with the bookstore manager to come up with a format that would suit both of you.

Lingerie Shops

The same ideas can be applied to lingerie shops.

Decorate the counter with your stylish arrangement and leave business cards for the customers to put in their wallets as they buy their lingerie.

Talk to the store manager and arrange to offer discounts on your flowers with the purchase of their products, making a business arrangement that will suit you both.

Wine Stores

Sell your flowers at the local wine shop. Put them on consignment and keep refilling the bucket beside the counter.

Keep your business cards handy on the counter.

Again, negotiate with your store owner to instigate a joint promotional deal-a discount on flowers when buying a particular bottle of wine. Flowers, wine and candlelit dinners go together.

120. SHOWING OFF

Approach all furniture and lighting shops. The customers in these stores are only there because they are keen on beautifying their homes. These are the types of customers you need.

Leave brochures, flyers, business cards on the counter. Again, you could supply the stores with a sample of your work, to advertise your skill and grab the customer's attention.

You could also negotiate a deal with the owner that, on sale of particular items, the customer could receive a voucher or discount for your floral services. Alternatively, you could barter some of your flowers in exchange for their database. Write personal letters of introduction to these clients.

Approach hotels and motels and catch some customers when they are away from home. Hotels and motels pride themselves on their beautiful premises, and a vase of flowers on the counter is mandatory.

You will, of course, keep a pile of business cards beside the arrangement for interested customers to pick up and take home with them.

121. BE ATTRACTIVE

Get smart. Show off your stuff. Let them see what you have got and what you do. Being in business is not the time to be timid. Shake off any shadows of shyness.

How can you attract attention?

Use local bulletin boards to post announcements about your business. Use tear-off slips so people do not need to write down any information. You want people to react on impulse and put your name into their pocket. Do not make it difficult for them to do this. Get the signs printed or word-process them yourself on your PC, add relevant graphics if you can-stylized flowers, valentine's hearts-to make it eye-catching and attract attention. Remember, you are striving for a professional image, as you expect to be paid as a professional.

Use your car. You are driving around in a mobile billboard sign. Use this to your advantage. You already have to travel from points A to B to deliver flowers, so it does not cost a cent more to get out there and let people see your name. Think of it as getting your name up in lights. It may not be Broadway, but it certainly is your own show, so it is up to you to make it work.

Get a good-quality sign made up and attach it to your car, remembering to include your business name, telephone number and a brief headline of what you do, your specialty service or approach. If you are not able to attach a sign to your car, then consider the magic of magnetic signs-magnets will do the same job without any hassle. Now do not forget to park your car in places where it will be noticed, and keep it tidy!

Encourage gossip. Good, positive gossip from your customers about your services is the best form of advertising you can get. Word-of-mouth promotion from your satisfied customers is invaluable, and certainly worth rewarding. Consider offering a bunch of flowers free after an existing customer of yours brings in two new customers to your business. Place a discreet sign on the counter to let them know you are offering this reward, or offer it in person to your regular customers.

Make friends. Join up with compatible businesses in your area and agree to refer clients between you.

123. WINNERS ARE GRINNERS

There are many organizations that run raffles. And every raffle needs a prize. What better way to advertise your florist shop than by donating a raffle prize?

Have a rubber stamp made that says "Happy to Help with Fund-raisers", and stamp it on your invoice. The prize would need to be at a value with which you feel comfortable. Ask that the name of your business be printed on all raffle tickets and say that you would like to be present at the draw to choose the winning ticket.

Request that there also be a photograph in the local newspaper, featuring you with the winner. A large photograph of you with a cheesy grin handing over your well-designed bunch of flowers will do wonders for your business. Imagine the advertising you have bought- for the price of a bunch of flowers.

Photo opportunities in the newspaper are a highly sought-after form of marketing, and what better form of print advertising can there be than one that is distributed to such an extensive portion of the community, and at the same time is free? In addition, this form of advertising is not really perceived as advertising by the majority of readers, as it appears under the guise of news.

The fund-raising organization is paying the printing costs-to feature the name of your enterprise on the raffle tickets. The name of your business is being disseminated throughout the community on each ticket that is sold. Even the people who do not buy a ticket will hear the name of your venture. And your presence at the draw will mean you are able to market yourself and your trade, to meet more potential clients.

The prize winner has clear potential to become a new customer. And you can bet that in their excitement they will be telling all their friends about their win. Add to that the fact that whenever someone comments about their prize, the name of your business will be on their lips.

This approach brings the possibility of winning not just one new customer but hundreds. And imagine the potential for advertising your business if you donate to more than one organization. Good, positive, gutsy advertising of this nature can only boost your profit.

You could consider donating a gift voucher rather than an actual bunch of flowers. All of the above still applies. In addition the winner has to visit your store to redeem their voucher, giving them a chance to look around and possibly make another purchase.

Study each request for donations or support to see whether it is something in which you believe strongly. Is it a legitimate cause? Is it too controversial and might alienate your customers?

123. ATTENTION SEEKING TACTICS

Why do not you try the following?

Talk: Volunteer to speak in your area of expertise to interested groups. Do not try to sell anything, just be there to spark people's curiosity. This is easier than you may imagine at first.

Think about your target market, the people you would expect to be your clients. Where do these people go for relaxation and recreation? What are their hobbies and interests? What clubs and societies would they belong to? Now, within these areas there will undoubtedly be groups, clubs and societies that host information evenings or social events. Get involved.

Most often there are groups just dying for a speaker. These are captive audiences for you and potential customers that will translate into $$$ for your business. Think laterally and cast the net wide.

Consider library and book groups, sports groups, business lunch groups, mothers' groups and nursing homes/homes for the aged. Even if these people are not interested in your services themselves, they will have friends and family members who might be. People will talk, and this is great for business.

Write: Approach your local newspaper or suburban magazine and offer to write a weekly column on your area of expertise. Also consider local radio and regional television stations: they are often looking for experts to host and present topics of interest. Offer to do this free. Remember, this is your advertising budget and it is many, many times more valuable than what you would otherwise have paid for. Make your article or session informative and entertaining. Do not do the hard sell here. What you are doing is establishing a fantastic reputation for yourself so that clients will be drawn to you.

Network You have heard it before, you have done it before, but the word still sounds a little scary. Relax! You know what you have to do, join groups and talk to people. Contact your local chamber of commerce or industry association and identify local businesses and groups you might be able to target.

Call the contact person and explain what you do and what your interests are, always considering how you could complement and help each other. Look up the "Clubs" section of your local telephone directory and make a few telephone calls to the club secretary; find out when their next meeting is and go along as a potential new member. Join if you can but make sure the group is worthy of your investment before you sign on. Remember, you are not there to sell your services directly; you are there to make friends and contacts.

Make sure you go armed with an excellent business card. Hand out your cards at every opportunity.

Each time you meet a new person, hand them a card and introduce yourself. If a conversation results, and it probably will, this is your opportunity to market yourself and your business. Take advantage of it. Work out beforehand what you will say and what points you want to get across. Prepare a 30-second introduction, outlining who you are, what you do and how your business benefits others. Remember, people tend to do business with people they know.

Be a sponsor: This need not cost you a lot. Think in terms of services you can provide. Sponsor a sports team; become the provider of flowers for their awards nights. In return, ask them to include your name in the sports program. Ask them to mention your sponsorship and support during the game on the loudspeaker or PA system. In this way, the spectators will be able to see that you are a professional and some of their loyalty for the team will spill over to you.

You now have four tips to gather publicity and attention without a huge advertising budget. Implement them now and use them to your advantage. Start today, it really is that simple.

124. FREEBIES

Everybody loves a freebie. But offer your low-cost freebies along with a customer purchase. Do it whenever you can, but always with an ulterior motive in mind. Let them take away a gift that will advertise your business.

Here are some ideas:
- Free telephone and address books, jotter pads, flower presses, framed pictures, business card holders, post-it notes-all with your business name, address and phone number beautifully

inscribed after purchase.
- Extra flowers in the bunch (after purchase)-or, with larger purchases, a small, cheerful, accompanying posy-with your business card prominently attached. That way your flowers end up advertising themselves in two locations.
- Free vases (with your business name and phone number tastefully inscribed).
- Free T-shirts (with your business name and phone number). This would depend on the size of your business and your resources. Select key individuals in your community or customers who buy from you on a regular basis or who have made a particularly large purchase. Or double up by using your T-shirts as an informal part of your uniform-on Fridays, perhaps, or while running deliveries.

Run a competition and give away flowers for:
- The Best Mum-for Mother's Day,
- The Best Grandmother,
- Teacher of the Month,
- Secretary of the Month,
- Most Caring Nursing Sister.

The list is endless. Nomination sheets can be available from your store, wherever your flowers are sold, or in the local newspaper. Make the most of the competition with a photo opportunity in the local newspaper.

A picture of you presenting "The Best Grandmother/Teacher" with a beautiful bunch of flowers and a big kiss on the cheek is great publicity for your business.

125. KEEP IT USEFUL

If you are going to invest money in merchandise advertising your business name with the specific purpose of giving it away free in a promotional special, make sure the product is going to serve some use to the customer. If it does not they will throw it away, and you lose your money.

126. SHOW YOUR GOODWILL

A personal visit to a business that has just opened, changed premises or renovated is a positive move. Wish them well in their new venture and present them with a small bunch of flowers in a vase with your logo imprinted. You are leaving behind a memento of your business, not only for your business colleagues but also for their clients or customers.

This will create an awareness of your business, both for your current customers and for potential new ones. Your business profile is being raised, so colleagues in complementary businesses will scramble to join you in any mutual promotional activities you dream up.

127. FREQUENT BUYING

Most people are familiar with the frequent buying (or loyalty) system. The concept is an oldie but a goldie, and is worthy of mention. All retail and service industries have found that those who sign up on the frequent-buyer program increase the rate at which they purchase. In addition, it reduces defection to other businesses.

Why does this have such strong customer appeal? It is the old get something for nothing syndrome. For example:

- Buy 10 bunches of flowers, get the 11th bunch free.
- Buy 10 bunches of flowers; receive 50% off next purchase.

Once customers are approaching purchase number 10, this gives them an extra incentive to buy a bunch of flowers for when the visitors come. And it discourages them from buying the bouquet they need for a gift at some other florist that catches their eye as they walk past. They know that they are on their way to receiving a discount at your florist, so they will make the extra effort to get there.

You could even give your customers a card to get stamped or punched each time they purchase a bunch of flowers, so that they are reminded each time they see it in their wallet that there are only two more purchases until they get their free bunch. You would need to get a unique stamp or hole punch that you could identify as your own.

128. BECOME A VIP

Everyone likes rewards. As children, we liked to receive a pat on the back, a gold star or a special treat. As adults, nothing has changed.

Reward your regular customers. Make them feel special. Make them feel welcome. Make them VIPs. And give them a card that says so.

Awarding VIP status at your store recognizes the customers' value not only to you but also to themselves.

Of course, part of being a VIP is receiving a 10% discount. Customers will feel important and receive a discount too!

But do not hand out the cards indiscriminately or they will lose their importance. Save them for the regular customers, the big buyers, or for your initial customers if you have just opened a new store.

Make the card look important. Print the letters VIP in large gold lettering on the front of the card. On the back, print:

(Insert name) is entitled to receive a 10% discount on purchase at (name of your store). Then sign it personally.

CHAPTER SUMMARY

Now that you have finished this chapter you should have an understanding of the following low cost big impact ways to promote your business:

- Making your mark
- Make the most of early morning traffic

- Winners are grinners
- Finding houses for your flowers
- Business arrangements
- Joining forces with other businesses
- Goodwill, frequent buyers and VIPs
- And many more

End of chapter six (6).

7 MAKE MONEY ANSWERING THE TELEPHONE
Telephone Techniques

How many phone calls do you receive each day that involve potential customers enquiring about price? Do you tell them the price immediately? Do they then say "Thank you very much, I'll get back to you" and hang up?

Many florists receive these calls, and many potential clients take the information away and never come back. Good business sense should tell you not to let them get away! When the client makes contact with you, make the most of it.

In this chapter you will find hints, tips and tricks on how to sell more using the telephone including:

- How to handle the "How much" question;
- Sell to the customer while they are on hold
- Use your answering machine/voicemail to generate business

Start selling more and talking less on the telephone now!

129. HOW MUCH IS THAT FLOWER

When you receive a phone call, try not to give out price information immediately because you will lose the opportunity to convince the potential client about the other positive aspects of your service. You might explain, encourage and build up the service to your heart's content, but the client will not be open to this information because their mind will still be centered on the cost.

Is cost the only thing that concerns the client about selecting a florist? Is the florist's artistic direction or techniques worthy of discussion? And is the florist's personal manner a chief factor? So, are you friendly? Do you really listen to their needs?

You need to open the lines of communication and build a rapport with the caller to impart this information. So chat with them. Take the emphasis away from giving out information. Redirect your thought processes to converting enquiries into sales, just like a salesman. You are aiming to build the value of the service first. Let the customer know exactly what they will be receiving.

Ask the client whether they have attended your shop before. This is another way to chat with the caller, to establish rapport and to make a sale all at the same time. Why do you need to know whether they are a regular client? Because if they are not already, your task is to make them one! Choose from some ideas below:

- If they have not attended before, tell them it is your policy to offer a discount to new customers.
- Tell them all new customers will receive a discount during the current month.
- Offer them a complimentary consultation, without obligation, where you can discuss their needs and their lifestyle.

After you do tell the potential customer the price of the service, do not pause. Move the conversation away from the price and towards action, giving the caller less time to feel uncomfortable, compare, analyze and back out.

In short, look at every telephone enquiry as a potential customer. Do not give a simple one-sentence response to a question. Let them see how friendly, cooperative and caring you are. Let them feel that they can trust you, that they will get value for money and quality service. Chances are they will not be able to resist.

130. HOLD THE LINE, PLEASE

Everyone has seen sitcoms or television commercials where the owners of the newly opened business are patiently waiting for customers to arrive. The phone finally rings. They rush to answer it, bowling each other over in the process. Do not do it.

Let the phone ring-for a short while (but no more than five rings). It looks as if you are busy. And if you are busy, the potential customer will think that lots of people must be buying from you. If the business is popular, you must be good. But never let the phone ring out.

Try putting your potential client on hold for a moment. Why? To show the customer your store must be busy. But do not leave them too long, or you will try your customer's patience. They will become frustrated, hang up and go elsewhere. It is a delicate balance.

131. ADS ON HOLD

While your customer is on hold, play relaxing or classical music. This is compatible with your floral theme, adds a touch of class and relaxes your customer. Relaxed people are more apt to buy.

Better still, you can also use the time to advertise your upcoming promotions, your fabulous service and dedication to customers. Mention the latest course in floral design that you have attended, the award you won. Talk about the specials, the sales, the retail items.

Hearing the voice of the owner builds a connection with the client, laying the foundations for future buying.

Use your answering machine to help you. It is an in-house, low-cost, 24-hour-a-day communication tool. Record a message similar to the one you have for putting customers on hold. Keep it short and allow them to leave a message for you if necessary. But change the message according to the current promotion you are running, or to mention any others that you have coming up.

When recording a message for an answering machine, ensure that the greeting is short but very professional. Write it down and practise it several times before recording.

CHAPTER SUMMARY

Now that you finished this chapter you should have an understanding of the following:

- How to handle the "How much" question.
- Sell to the customer while they are on hold.
- Use your answering machine/voicemail to generate business.

End of chapter seven (7).

8 TIME IS MONEY
Strategies for television and radio advertising

Television advertising, done well, is a highly effective way to market your florist shop. It enables you to reach your audience direct; it positions your business as an entity in your community; and it gives you prestige.

The visual element is your best advertising tool. Research shows that most people remember pictures and faces more easily than they remember names, words or slogans.

But television advertising can be expensive. Choosing to run your commercial just once in prime time can blow your whole budget.

In this chapter you will find hints, tips strategies and advice on advertising on television and radio.

Start making sound waves now!

132. REPEAT REPEAT REPEAT

Advertising of any kind needs to be repeated. It is not enough to run an ad once or twice. It should be constant. The same applies to television advertising. It is not enough to play your commercial once and then expect people to remember it.

133. TIME IS MONEY

The timeslot in which you choose to air your commercial can be the most expensive element of television advertising, and therefore potentially the most cost-prohibitive.

A way to repeat your commercial, and not blow your budget, is to choose less expensive spots. Check with your local station to find out when their cheaper times are.

You also need to consider the actual television show in which you select to air your commercial. Not only will it affect the cost of your advertising program but it must be both a show and a time slot that is targeted at your audience. The advertising salesperson will be able to help you. Television stations know who watches what, when.

The smaller the television audience, the lower the advertising rate. You can cash in on this fact and choose to advertise predominantly during the day to attract the home-maker, designing your commercials with an interior decorating angle. Or perhaps give them a family orientation. You may well be able to negotiate a package, whereby most of your slots are during the daytime but a smaller selection fall just before and after prime time, to capture other sectors of the market.

You can choose to advertise more heavily just before traditional flower giving occasions.

134. THE PLACE WHERE YOU LIVE

The cost of television advertising will depend on the area in which you choose to advertise. It is much less expensive to buy air time on rural television stations than with city broadcasters. The more potential viewers in a time slot or region, the more you can expect to pay to reach them.

While television advertising can be expensive, if you use it to capture the exact market you aim for it can be worth it. And if you choose your times wisely you can build your business to a point that television spots in prime time viewing might well become a business reality.

CHAPTER SUMMARY

Now that you have finished reading this chapter, you should have an understanding of the following:

- Whether to run your ad once or more
- Whether to advertise in prime time
- Different locations affect pricing.

End of chapter eight (8)

9 SOCIAL MONEY
Use social media platforms to grow your business

Social media is an effective way to connect with customers.

There almost as many social media sites as there are types of flowers with new ones popping up every day! To discuss a social media strategy for each of them would make for a very long book. So this chapter will focus on four (4) tried and true social media platforms.

In this chapter you will find hints, tips strategies and advice to grow your business using the following social media platforms:

- Facebook,
- Twitter,
- Instagram,
- Pinterest

Get social now!

135. KEEP IT SOCIAL

The most important thing to remember when marketing with social media is the word **social**. People are not using these platforms to be inundated with advertising or getting messages from hundreds of businesses. Do not use the hard sell. Use good, interesting content and do not pressure people.

136. FACEBOOK ME

Love it or hate it, Facebook is currently the world's biggest social network. It can raise awareness of your florist and get people excited about flowers. You can also use it to get people to buy flowers more frequently.

Follow these tips for Facebook success:

- Have a great profile photo, it will set the tone for your page. Try a photo of your best flower arrangement.
- Use the cover photo to showcase more of your arrangements, or

to showcase your shop.
- Post photos of your arrangements on a regular basis. Remember to include photos from all your price brackets. You want your followers and customers to think they can afford to purchase your flowers frequently.
- Post information. Post information on how to look after flowers, flow of the month, or flower meaning.

The more information you can give away online, the more people will look forward to your posts. Writing quick informative posts that educate your followers will reinforce your knowledge and professional skills.

You could write about the following topics:
- How to design a wedding bouquet
- How to select a florist for your wedding
- How to care for your flowers
- The language of flowers

Get people excited about flowers. Do not stick to regular bouquets; instead come up with specific gift ideas.

Come up with an everyday "I was just thinking about you" bouquet. Post the photo on your wall, and ask something like, "Was thinking about an arrangement that simply tells someone that you are thinking of them... thoughts? Suggestions?"

Or try simple and budget-friendly. Come up an inexpensive 6-stem bouquet and suggest that your fans tell someone that they love them today. You never know, you might make some wives very happy and then they become customers as well.

Monthly contests

Running a contest on your Facebook page is a great way to attract followers to your site. Here are some ideas:
- Host a monthly flower contest for fans of your Facebook page.
- Mother's Day contest for people to submit 250 words about how great their mother is, Teachers day, Administrative professional day, and any other day you care to promote. Remember they are all reasons for people to buy your flowers.
- Think up can all be an excuse to run a Facebook contest.

137. TWITTER

The world's second largest social network allows users to post 140-character updates ("tweets") which are shared with their followers.
- Post news, share links, answer questions.
- Post information about flowers, very similar to what you post on Facebook i.e. flower of the month, flower meanings, how to care for floral arrangements.

- Promote your monthly contest.
- Use custom and popular tags to establish brand values.
- Be active in following and retweeting others.

138. INSTAGRAM

Instagram is a visual medium so use it to visually promote your business with great photos of any of the following.

- Post photos of your arrangements from all your price brackets. Remember you want your followings to think they can afford to buy flowers frequently
- Also post photos of any events you might provide flowers for (i.e. weddings, corporate events) - with the organizers permission of course!)
- Photo of contestant winners and their prize (with their permission of course).
- Photos of any non-floral products you sell
- Seasonal products e.g. Christmas floral arrangements

139. PINTEREST

Pinterest allows users to pin websites, recipes, photos, and maps to virtual pin boards. These boards can be accessed by other users via a feed or search, or boards can be kept private.

Use Pinterest the same way you would use Instagram; promote your business with great photos of any of the following.

- Post photos of your arrangements from all your price brackets. Remember you want your followings to think they can afford to buy flowers frequently
- Also post photos of any events you might provide flowers for (i.e. weddings, corporate events) - with the organizers permission of course!)
- Photo of contestant winners and their prize (with their permission of course).
- Photos of any non-floral products you sell
- Seasonal products e.g. Christmas floral arrangements

CHAPTER SUMMARY

This chapter contained hints, tips strategies and advice to grow your business using the following social media platforms:

- Facebook,
- Twitter,
- Instagram,
- Pinterest

End chapter nine (9).

THRIVE
Survive and thrive for years to come.

10 RIGHT ON THE MONEY
Keys to long term success

Wow! You have followed all the advice laid out in this book and hopefully have a thriving business.

In this final chapter, you will learn some strategies to keep your business thriving for many years to come.

When you have finished this chapter, you should have an understanding of the following concepts to manage your business.

- Make a statement
- The importance of planning
- The importance of the budget
- The calendar of events

Start planning to stay a little bit longer now!

140. MAKE A STATEMENT

A mission statement can give your business focus and help to clarify, and thus reach goals.

A mission statement is a one-sentence statement that encapsulates the philosophy of your florist. For example, "Flower Power aims to . . ."etc.

If you are a small florist not a big organization, do you really need one? The answer is yes.

A mission statement gives your business direction and cohesion. When decisions need to be made and the choice of which way to go is not clear, it will help to return to your mission statement.

Determine the niche that your florist business will fill. For example:

- Who is your target market?
- What are their needs?
- What is your goal?

- What are your strengths and weaknesses?
- Who is your chief competitor?
- What are their strengths and weaknesses?
- What is your competitor's target market?

To develop your own mission statement and to make things clear, complete the following:

The purpose of (insert your business name) is to.......

The target market will be....

The purpose will be achieved by positioning the flower service in the following way....

Marketing tools to be used will be...

Cost of marketing will be $....

When you have completed your mission statement, use it like a roadmap to see where you are going. When you can see where you are going you can monitor your progress towards your destination.

141. HERE TODAY, GONE TOMORROW

Every business and marketing guru will tell you that you must spend money advertising and marketing your business.

"But I'm a small florist business. Why should I?" you ask "I haven't really got the money to spend. Besides, how do you know it works? And anyway, I advertise now and then, when I think of it. Or when I can afford it. Won't that do?" In a word: no. Here are some reasons why:

- The market is constantly changing.
- People forget
- People will spend where they are told
- Strengthen your position
- Make new customers; and
- Keep your old customers

The market is constantly changing. Think about the families who move out of town. What about those who move into town? Think of the youngsters who will grow into adults, get married, and have babies. You need to constantly market your business because the world is not static.

People forget. Sad but true. Research indicates that only 63% of readers remembered brand names and specific advertising after a 13-week campaign. One month after that same campaign, only 32% of respondents could recall the brand advertising message. You must keep telling them who you are, where you are, and what you offer.

People will spend where they are told. Customers need to buy. You have to tell them you have what they want. How else will they know? If customers are not reminded of your business, they will spend their money with another florist.

Strengthen your position. People are attracted to strength. Customers like stability. Look solid, established, known. They like stability. Your flower stop will attract people if it has been around for a period of time and enjoys a good reputation, built up over years of marketing. If it is new, the marketing approach you employ can give it a feeling of good, solid backing.

Make new customers. You cannot start a business without marketing. It shows that you exist.

Keep your old customers. It costs five to seven times more to get new customers than it costs to retain them. But even your regulars will become bored with your routine, be poached by someone else or just plain forget about you-unless you refresh their memories.

The best customers are those who have adopted regular visits to their florist as a lifestyle habit. But customers will not assume this role by themselves. You need to help them.

142. CALENDAR OF EVENTS

A marketing calendar is an essential tool for maximizing your profit. Without it you will drift along, week by week, hoping to make money and miss your opportunities for making more profit.

Think of the different types of marketing strategies available to you. Choose the ones that are compatible, that you are able to employ and to use regularly.

Make a promotions calendar using the following steps:
- a) Work out when your quiet times of the year are, and plan promotions for those spots.
- b) Work out how many promotions you will need for the year.
- c) Work on promotion concepts for the quiet times.
- d) Look at your past successful promotions and repeat them. Also look at other companies' successful campaigns. What made them stand out? Can you replicate it?
- e) Look at your past not-so-successful promotions and see what you can learn.
- f) Stagger your marketing techniques. Avoid using blocks of advertising in only one medium.
- g) Change the lengths of your campaigns, to achieve a healthy balance.

But remember to allow periods during which there are no special sales, to give credibility to the sales that you do have.

Well laid plans are profitable investments of time, and will help you achieve your goals faster.

143. THE IMPORTANCE OF ADVERTISING AND MARKETING BUDGET

As a business owner it is important for you to track where your dollars are going, especially you're advertising and marketing dollars.

Keeping track of the expenditure shows how effective your advertising actually is, and helps you quantify advertising dollars with a rate of redemption (in simple speak, the percentage of sales you achieve per advertising dollar spent).

Money spent on marketing is a reinvestment in your business, so the closer to 5% of sales you can spend, the better. Of course, your other financial commitments will also affect whether you can allow for 5%.

For example, if your projected gross sales for the year were $200,000 your advertising budget would be $10,000.

This money is usually allocated to the traditional forms of media. You can also have a miscellaneous budget, to support non-traditional or creative forms of marketing to be implemented in a spur-of-the-moment style.

Break down your budget by media, focusing on those which are best suited to your geographic region (city or country) and the demographics (age, sex and income) of your target market. As an example of how to do this:

Direct mail: flyers 10c apiece x 10 000 = $1000
Radio: slots during drive time 100 X $50 = $5000
Television: one short regional ad campaign = $2000
Miscellaneous: promotional material not planned = $2000

(Note: The television budget will depend solely on the area you live in. This example has been based on a short campaign run in a regional area. City-based rates will differ from regional rates.)

The budgeting process allows you stick to a certain expenditure, and limits sporadic spending. All too often small businesses will under advertise until business starts to fall off, then overcompensate with a rushed campaign of panic advertising that costs too much.

The budget allows you to use a variety of media to target your market, also to measure the success of the advertising you undertake. It need not be a technical financial breakdown but rather a general spending plan for your advertising dollars. Do not start the year without one!

144. BUDGET BUDGET BUDGET

Save money and save your business-stick to a budget! The most common causes of failure in budgeting are: unrealistic goals; quitting too soon; and misunderstanding what a budget really is (i.e. a way of ensuring that your incomings are greater than your outgoings).

CHAPTER SUMMARY

Now that you have finished this chapter, you should have an understanding of the following concepts to manage your business.

- Make a statement
- The importance of planning & budgeting
- The calendar of events.

THE BUCK STOPS HERE
The final tip

145. HAVE FUN!

Whatever you choose to focus on in marketing your florist, remember it will all work better if you enjoy it. So take a light hearted approach and experiment with a range of promotions to get your name and image firmly established in the public eye.

Learn from everyone you can, whether it is national chains or local stores. Learn from business ides that work. Learn from business ideas that do not work. If it works, do more of it. If it does not work, learn from it. And remember your small florist can be a lot more flexible and responsive than a huge hierarchical corporation. So make this your small business advantage. Enjoy.

Good luck with your florist shop and thank you for reading this book.

REFERENCES

Forsyth, P. Marketing on a Tight Budget, Piatkus, London, 1993, pp. 128-9.
Gschwandtner, G. Selling Power, July/August 1998; 18: 6, p. 8.
Foley, M.D. The Motivated Salon, Milady Publishing, New York, 1997.
Caples, J. Tested Advertising Methods, Prentice Hall,
Englewood Cliffs, NJ, 1997, p. 13.
Mattimore, Bryan. 99% Inspiration: Tips, Tales and Techniques for Liberating Your Business, Amacom, New York, 1993.
The Marketing Globe, September 1999; 10: 9, p. 4.
Source: Independent research of people aged 18-64 conducted by DBM Consultants Pty Ltd.
Levinson, Jay Conrad. Guerrilla Marketing, Houghton Mifflin Company, Boston, MA, 1984, p. 143.

ABOUT THE AUTHOR

Brendan Power is the author of The Small Business Success Guide; a series of books on small business marketing and operations.

The Small Business Success Guides are written by Brendan with the input of small business owners.

A small business owner himself, Brendan was born in a pub. He grew up working in his father's hotels, then later in his father's brewery. In addition, Brendan has owned and operated a number of pubs in Australia and the United States of America.

Brendan also has extensive background in marketing. He has worked in the United States of America for an American based brewer and was Managing Director of a company that specialized in the management of hotels, restaurants and cafes. He was also the CEO of an international backpacking company.

He currently spends his time writing, consulting to small business owners and helping his wife with the school run.

Brendan has Bachelor of Business and an MBA and a graduate of the Australian Institute of Company Directors.

Made in the USA
Middletown, DE
17 July 2018